Prehistory, Personality, and Place

Emil W. Haury and the Mogollon Controversy

Jefferson Reid and Stephanie Whittlesey

T0168675

The University of Arizona Press   Tucson

The University of Arizona Press
© 2010 The Arizona Board of Regents
All rights reserved

www.uapress.arizona.edu

Library of Congress Cataloging-in-Publication Data

Reid, J. Jefferson
    Prehistory, personality, and place : Emil W. Haury and the
Mogollon controversy / Jefferson Reid and Stephanie
Whittlesey.
        p.   cm.
    Includes bibliographical references and index.
    ISBN 978-0-8165-2862-2 (hard cover)
    ISBN 978-0-8165-2863-9 (pbk.)
    1. Mogollon culture. 2. Southwest, New—Antiquities.
3. Archaeology—Southwest, New—History—20th century.
4. Haury, Emil W. (Emil Walter), 1904–1992.
5. Archaeologists—Southwest, New—Biography.
6. Archaeologists—Psychology—Case studies.
7. Geography—Psychological aspects—Case studies.
8. Cultural landscapes—Southwest, New—Case studies.
9. Point of Pines Site (Ariz.) 10. University of Arizona.
Archaeological Field School—History—20th century.
I. Whittlesey, Stephanie Michelle. II. Title.

E99.M76R455 2010
979'.01—dc22
2009035834

Publication of this book is made possible in part by a grant
from the Provost's Author Support Fund of the University
of Arizona.

Manufactured in the United States of America on acid-free,
archival-quality paper.

15   14   13   12   11   10   6   5   4   3   2   1

Contents

Figures

Preface

This book is about the history of the Mogollon controversy in Southwest archaeology—whether or not the ancient Mogollon culture was a distinctive cultural entity—and its resolution. It is a story that began in the mountains of New Mexico and ended in the mountains of Arizona, surely some of the most compelling places on earth. It also is about the remarkable individuals who discovered the Mogollon culture, fought to validate it, and eventually resolved the controversy. As such, our book is about places and personalities—the role of place in shaping the intellect and personalities of archaeologists, and the unusual intersections of personalities and places that produced resolutions of some intractable problems in Southwest history. Our book also is about discovery.

There was no flash of insight to mark the moment when we, as archaeologists, "discovered" the Mogollon in the form we now label Mogollon Pueblo (Reid and Whittlesey 1997, 1999, 2005). We had been working at the University of Arizona Archaeological Field School at Grasshopper Pueblo on the Fort Apache Indian Reservation since the early 1970s. At that time, William A. Longacre, professor of anthropology at the University of Arizona, was director of the field school, and the "New Archaeology" influenced us to the extent that we were far more interested in adaptive responses to environmental stress (Reid 1973, 1978) and developing middle-range theory for identifying material correlates of human behavior (Whittlesey 1978) than in cultural or ethnic identifications. This was shortly to change. Reid had always been deeply interested in the history of Southwest archaeology, and in the spring of 1975, he began interviewing Emil W. Haury, professor of anthropology at the University of Arizona and the discoverer and defender of the Mogollon, to compile an oral history. About the same time, Whittlesey began researching the Mogollon controversy. Sometime between the spring of 1975 and the fall of 1979, when the first draft of the Mogollon controversy was being cobbled together from Whittlesey's notes, we discovered that Grasshopper Pueblo fit Erik K. Reed's (1948, 1950) model for the Western Pueblo, or Mogollon

Pueblo. Furthermore, those aspects of Grasshopper lifeways and material culture that did not fit his model allowed us to develop the concept of ethnic coresidence—people of different cultural traditions living together in the same pueblo community. Reed's model permitted us to identify the coresidence of Mogollon and Anasazi, or Ancestral Pueblo (Reid and Whittlesey 1982, 1999), long before sophisticated chemical techniques were developed to support these conclusions (Ezzo and Price 2002).

The genesis of this book lies, therefore, not only in oral history and literature reviews but in real-life archaeological techniques for answering questions about ancient life. We discovered a model that fit the facts of Grasshopper Pueblo as we knew them. In our book *Grasshopper Pueblo: A Story of Archaeology and Ancient Life* (Reid and Whittlesey 1999), we present our interpretation of Mogollon Pueblo ecology, sociology, and ideology as revealed by thirty years of archaeological research in the Grasshopper region. Although this was not our ultimate intent, the book resembles in format and content a sequel to another archaeological recollection. This was Paul Sidney Martin's *Digging into History: A Brief Account of Fifteen Years of Archaeological Work in New Mexico* (1959), written for a general audience as a summary of Mogollon culture history in the Pine Lawn Valley.

Regrettably, Haury did not live to comment on our ethnography of the Grasshopper Mogollon, but we know that he was never comfortable with this association of Grasshopper with an unqualified Mogollon label. Haury did, however, accept the label we use here: "A useful descriptive compromise label for the communities in the eleventh century and later that contain features of both cultures is Mogollon-Pueblo, first suggested by Joe Ben Wheat in 1955. It is less acceptable to call them Mogollon, glossing over the highly indicative and readily identifiable attributes that spell an Anasazi heritage" (Haury 1985a:404). We concur wholeheartedly, even though we, like many others, have employed *Mogollon* as a shorthand label on maps and in narrative sketches for cultural variability spread out over twelve centuries in the central mountains of Arizona and New Mexico. Strictly speaking, as we will discuss, *Mogollon* should apply to the mountain people living in pit houses until around AD 1000, and *Mogollon Pueblo* to those descendants living in masonry pueblos.

Perhaps the most compelling reason for writing this book derived from our simple wonder, as mature archaeologists with decades of experience in processual, behavioral, and post-processual archaeology, at how the Mogollon controversy could have originated in the first place (see Reid and Whittlesey 2005 for a discussion of these different archaeologies). These debates certainly persist in twenty-first-century archaeology, but they seldom, if ever, center on such apparently simplistic and easily accepted concepts as archaeological cultures. This bemusement, in turn, led us to consider "Doc" Haury's role in the controversy and its conclusion.

We note that this is not a biography of Haury, although it borrows liberally from his own autobiographical writings and biographical sketches by others. Indeed, we consider him to be a remarkable archaeologist, teacher, and scholar, but the full disclosure of his personal story awaits another time and perhaps other observers.

The heart of our story lies in the arguments and actions surrounding the Mogollon discovery, definition, and debate. Haury set the controversy in motion with his fieldwork in New Mexico and his definition of the Mogollon culture. He also orchestrated the closure of the first and most dramatic stage of the debate in the 1950s through his personal approach to controversy—the collection of new evidence—and by the judicious application of academic power. We catalog this strategy in several chapters that explore facets of the debate as they were carried out at different times and places and by various scholars. We discuss the fact that during the 1960s and 1970s, a "New Archaeology" shifted attention away from the research questions of cultural affiliation and antiquity that had been at the heart of the Mogollon controversy. By 1980, a biennial Mogollon Conference initiated a new era of research, questioning, and controversy concerning the Mogollon, but this time without Haury's participation.

When the facts and the anecdotes are bundled together, they present a rather compelling picture of an academician who was sincerely interested in understanding the unwritten past, who believed wholeheartedly in the techniques and models of scientific archaeology as it was understood at that time, and who used position and influence to assist scholarship, rather than as a means of self-promotion or administrative advancement. We believe we can see clearly the influence of place not only in molding Haury's personality, but also in orchestrating a solution to the controversy. The Mogollon could not have been defended more staunchly or more effectively at a place other than Point of Pines. Most strikingly, it was the way in which Haury handled the Mogollon controversy and his chosen techniques for resolving it—cordial debate coupled with a staunch stand and an unwavering belief that the way to resolve arguments was to collect fresh, new data—that exemplify his personality.

It is a testimony to the complexity of the Mogollon controversy and its participants that this book took decades to complete. Our acknowledgments are equally complex. Loren Haury, Raymond Thompson, and Carol Gifford took time from their busy lives to review the manuscript thoroughly—Carol from an editorial perspective; Ray from the vantage of an archaeologist who knew the debate's participants and had an intimate knowledge of the places on the Mogollon landscape, particularly Point of Pines; and Loren as Haury's son. Jan Danson Haury graciously shared photographs of her father and thoughts on her father-in-law. Loren's and Jan's comments, insights, and pictures from the family album were invaluable. We regret that Agnese Nelms Haury was unable to review the manuscript.

We also wish to thank the staff of the Mennonite Library and Archives at Bethel College in North Newton, Kansas, who helped us to locate photographs and other information about the Haury family. We learned firsthand what Mennonite lives and landscapes were like in nineteenth-century Kansas from the Kauffman Museum affiliated with Bethel College, the Mennonite Heritage Museum in Goessel, Kansas, and the Tallgrass Prairie National Preserve on the edge of the Flint Hills.

We also appreciate the assistance of the staff of the Laboratory of Anthropology at Santa Fe, who helped us explore the Pecos Conference Archives. We are always grateful to the helpful staff of the Arizona State Museum. Alan Ferg, archivist, assisted Erin O'Meara in tracking the 1931 survey through the archives, and Rebecca Donnelly and George Michael Jacobs assisted with the figures gleaned from the photographic collections. Stephen Nash at the Denver Museum of Nature and Science provided the photograph of Paul Martin and John Rinaldo reproduced here, courtesy the Field Museum of Natural History. Thanks also go to Christine Szuter and Allyson Carter of the University of Arizona Press and the editors and other magicians who turn words into books. Two anonymous reviewers offered excellent suggestions for revisions. The office of the Provost of the University of Arizona assisted publication with an award through the Author Support Fund. Brandon Gabler provided invaluable technical support.

Last, we owe the greatest debt of gratitude to Emil Haury himself. As teacher, mentor, and colleague, he offered a model of the renaissance archaeologist after which we strove to fashion ourselves. He was the consummate "field man," but he also had an extraordinary intellect, gentlemanly ways, and legendary ability to advance the goals of anthropology at the University of Arizona. We miss him, and our ultimate wish is that he would be proud of the story we tell here.

1
Prehistory, Personality, and Place

> In simple language, what one did to expand the horizons of
> understanding of the human past had to be bereft of guile,
> pretense, selfishness, and ego. Although one strived to do his best
> and hoped for recognition, the rewards for high achievement
> came naturally through honest peer recognition.
>
> —Emil Haury (1995:720)

This book traces the history of the Mogollon controversy in Southwest archaeology and the role that Emil W. Haury—discoverer and definer of the Mogollon culture—played in resolving that controversy. Haury was not a flamboyant archaeologist, and his archaeology lacked the temples, tombs, and treasures that most people associate with the thrill of archaeological discovery. His contributions to our understanding of the ancient past in the Southwest, however, are arguably the most significant of the twentieth century. Our story is about archaeology—undoubtedly a highly romanticized profession that conjures notions of gold and ghosts—and about discovery. Our theme, however, is to present the real archaeologist behind the real archaeology—the archaeology that fashions from dirt, potsherds, and pit houses a true understanding of the people of the prehistoric past, not just the artifacts they left behind and that fill museum shelves. Our story goes behind the scenes to paint a more complete picture of what archaeological discovery is *really* about. Often, the pictures of past times and places we toil to create are unremarkable for anything other than being a piece of the human experience, but that does not make them any less valuable.

How *do* archaeologists come to know the unwritten past through the study of the material objects left behind? The popular perception of archaeology is one of a series of artifact discoveries, that, when pieced together, give the past its special shape and character. Many people believe that archaeological discoveries are ruled by chance and the special karma of the gifted and persistent explorer, who often lacks professional training. Once located, the archaeological find is painstakingly uncovered with dental pick and brush, meticulously reconstructed, and ultimately displayed for the public to behold.

Without question, there are monumental breakthroughs in archaeology, such as the discovery of the Rosetta Stone and the decipherment of Mayan glyphs, but they are discoveries that transcend artifacts because they enable archaeologists to reconstruct the ancient past. In the Southwest, the monumental archaeological breakthrough was the discovery of tree-ring dating and, for much of the rest of the world, it was the development of radiocarbon dating. These discoveries allowed archaeologists to make sense of the record by placing it in absolute time. As in all historical sciences, advances in knowledge come about through the diligent pursuit of answers to appropriate questions by creative investigators.

We wish to frame the archaeological enterprise as similar to other disciplines that probe the unknown, that seek to understand a past time that cannot be seen, just as physicists seek to model the elemental but invisible structures and forces of the universe. Most nonprofessionals think that discovery is a one-time thing: the archaeologist digs something up, writes an academic paper about it, puts the artifacts in a museum, and the story comes to a close. The archaeology of our story, however, is one of ongoing process.

Our story also is one of controversy, and this also goes against the popular perception of archaeology. Most nonprofessionals think that archaeological discovery is not subject to dispute; once something has been discovered, it is accepted as reality by all, once and for all. Whereas this may well be true of objects—there can be little dispute about a pot or a pueblo or a canopic jar—it is emphatically not true for ideas, inferences, and reconstructions of the past. Prehistory is the product of evaluating data and inference, and different archaeologists have distinct approaches. Archaeology is by nature multivocal, shaped by argument, and open to controversy. Because archaeological interpretations are the product of a fragmentary record of the past, any increments of evidence open the door for new interpretations that challenge old ones and fuel the possibilities for controversy.

Our theme, then, is to tell the unwritten, behind-the-scenes tale of a true archaeological discovery—an intangible one, relating a particular idea about the past—and how this discovery was disputed, argued, and eventually justified by a group of scholars working in the early years of Southwest archaeology. The discovery was that of the Mogollon culture, an ancient group of Native Americans who lived in what is today the mountain Transition Zone of east-central Arizona and western New Mexico. The discoverer was Haury, surely the preeminent archaeologist of his day. The controversy was whether the Mogollon culture was a valid, distinctive cultural entity or simply a backwoods variant of the better-known Ancestral Pueblo, or Anasazi, culture. Our tale centers on how archaeologists gain knowledge of prehistory—the unwritten past—through academic discourse within the body of thoughts and theories constituting Western science and historical inquiry. Specifically, we discuss at length how archaeologists learn about the unwritten past by studying material items and their associations in time and space.

Within our general theme, we explore the concatenation of personality and place in shaping a major controversy in the history of Southwest archaeology and its successful resolution. How did Haury, who defined many of the Southwest's ancient cultures and wrote prolifically about them, come to assume such a significant and productive position? What factors shaped Haury's personality and the academic power that he held? We propose that, in part, places shaped Haury's view and intellectual style. In arguing this point, we will cross vast expanses of midwestern prairie, the rugged mountains of Arizona and New Mexico, and the Sonoran Desert landscape where Haury spent his formative professional years and the remainder of his career at the University of Arizona.

Personality and Place

We are convinced of the power of place to shape personalities and cultures. People interact with places, and by these interactions, the ways they view their natural and social environments, and their spiritual connections with the land and its inhabitants, they create cultural landscapes. In turn, people are shaped by these places of their own creation. For more than fifty years, anthropologists, cultural geographers, and archaeologists have explored this approach to understanding human-environment interactions, which has been called the cultural-landscape perspective (Ashmore and Knapp 1999; Basso 1996; Jackson 1984; Whittlesey 2003). Our thesis is that many ineffable aspects of Haury's personality were the product of his birthplace on the icy plains of Kansas and the romantic but hard-edged spaces of the Southwest to which he immigrated—the

rugged mountains of Arizona and New Mexico, the stunning but bru-
tally hot Sonoran Desert, but most especially, the woods and prairies of
Point of Pines. Place not only shaped personality, but it also molded the
archaeological answers to the Mogollon controversy, which was resolved
among the pit houses and pueblos of Point of Pines. This island of ancient
habitation located on the isolated San Carlos Apache Reservation in
east-central Arizona, where Haury directed the University of Arizona
Archaeological Field School, yielded an incomparably rich archaeological record that served Haury well in resolving the controversy.

There are multiple facets to Haury's extraordinary personality that
shaped his discovery of the Mogollon culture, his response to the controversy that the definition of the Mogollon generated, and his orchestration of a conclusion to the debate. One of the most important, we
believe, is the simple fact that Haury was sincerely interested in understanding the prehistoric past. We believe it was this interest that underscored his academic achievements and prompted his response to the
controversy.

Another aspect of his personality was the dimension of power, by
which we mean the capacity to influence belief and behavior. Haury grew
up in a midwestern Mennonite academic community providing ample
daily examples of authority and power in its selfless, minimalist expression. During the years that we knew him and in the many hours of oral-
history taping, we cannot recall any mention of power, perhaps because,
like intelligence and height, it was something Haury naturally possessed.
Any gaps could be filled in with the skills he acquired during apprentice-
ships under Byron Cummings, first director of the Arizona State Museum
and head of the Department of Archaeology at the University of Arizona; A. E. Douglass, astronomer and inventor of tree-ring dating; and
Harold S. Gladwin, the iconoclastic founder of Gila Pueblo Archaeological Foundation.

That said, we also observe that academic power, in part, gave Haury
the latitude to explore the Mogollon concept through the University of
Arizona Archaeological Field School and to direct student research toward
resolving the Mogollon controversy. In 1937, at the age of thirty-three,
Haury became head of the Archaeology Department, soon changed to
Anthropology, at the University of Arizona. The following year, he took
over as director of the Arizona State Museum. He held these dual positions throughout the prime of his academic career, finally throwing off
the yoke of administration to return to research in 1964 at age sixty. His

administrative positions gave him bureaucratic advantage, and his pres-
tigious Harvard doctorate provided additional leverage within the provin-
cial university community.

Personality also comes to play in the form of an ancillary cast of
characters. In addition to our central figure, a number of other archaeologists played out roles in this drama. Central were the archaeologists
of Harvard University, who led the charge against the Mogollon. Also
significant were the pro-Mogollonists who, like Haury, argued the integrity of the Mogollon culture with their shovels. We will discuss many
of these colorful and important figures, along with their contributions
on both sides of the controversy.

Defining Culture

Before we introduce the condensed version of the Mogollon controversy,
it may be worthwhile to pause to consider what we mean by the term
"culture" and why culture is important. Culture has been defined in many
different ways by anthropologists and archaeologists, and no doubt we
can expect further revisions and redefinitions. As archaeologists, we cannot define cultures as do ethnographers, because we are limited to material remains and lack information about important intangibles, such as
language. In archaeological terms, a culture is defined as a particular
constellation of traits distinguishable from those of other cultures, and
usually it is associated with a limited geographic distribution and often
with a particular "adaptation" to an environmental zone. The culture his-
torians of Haury's day had no illusions that they were digging up "cultures" in the anthropological sense; rather, they focused on the material
objects that could be used as identifying criteria—pottery types, architecture, projectile-point styles, and so on. It is on the basis of this definition of culture that the proponents argued the Mogollon culture to be
distinctive and separate from the other defined archaeological cultures
of the day.

We think culture still retains an important place in contemporary
archaeology, although a much different one from its role in the 1930s. We
argue that the archaeological use of culture and ethnicity is necessary
and falls securely within the contemporary anthropological concern with
identity (Mills 2004). All human groups make a clear distinction between
themselves and others, in language and in practice (Reid 1998:635–36).
Cultural, ethnic, and linguistic distinctions are real today, and there is

scant reason to doubt their reality prehistorically. Moreover, contemporary peoples categorize themselves according to cultural or ethnic groups with names in their own language that usually translate as "the People."

Culture and Controversy Condensed

The Mogollon culture was one of four major prehistoric cultures of the American Southwest, the others being the Ancestral Pueblo (Anasazi) of the Colorado Plateau, the Hohokam of the southern Arizona Sonoran Desert, and the lesser-known Patayan of the Arizona-California deserts along the Colorado River. The Mogollon were a mountain people of east-central Arizona and west-central New Mexico. Early in their history, their way of life resembled that of the Western Apache—they "moved like the wind" according to the seasons, searching out game and the fruits of wild-plant gathering that were the mainstay of their diet. In the centuries after AD 1000, the Mogollon became increasingly dependent on corn agriculture and came to resemble the Anasazi people with whom they would merge when their mountain homes were abandoned at the close of the fourteenth century.

The decades we spent at Grasshopper on the Fort Apache Reservation brought us into firsthand friendship with Apaches from the nearby community of Cibecue. Among the many effects of this association was getting to know an Apache way of living on the same kind of landscape that the prehistoric Mogollon inhabited. Our interpretations of Mogollon life took on a rather marked Apache cast, and much of the romanticism accorded the late-nineteenth-century warrior Apache was likewise transferred to the faceless Mogollon. This picture is not artificial, because there are real similarities that make the culturally and genetically unrelated mountain Apache an appropriate analog for the Mogollon. We could not hope for a more picturesque or romantic collage of cultural images.

Haury first glimpsed the mountain Mogollon in 1931 and fully defined the culture five years later in a publication of the Gila Pueblo Archaeological Foundation describing his excavations at two pit-house villages in western New Mexico—*The Mogollon Culture of Southwestern New Mexico*. Immediately, the concept of the Mogollon culture divided archaeologists of the day into two camps: those who accepted Haury's postulation of a separate culture and those who did not. A decade and a half later, in his discussion of the archaeology of the Petrified Forest region of northern Arizona, Fred Wendorf provided an eyewitness account and a succinct summary of the ongoing controversy and its major participants. He wrote:

> The Mogollon particularly has been the center of a protracted controversy. . . . Emil Haury, Harold Colton, John McGregor, Paul Martin, John Rinaldo, Ed Lehmer, and, until 1942, Harold Gladwin have contended that it was a "basic" culture from which the Anasazi and perhaps Hohokam received their stimulus for ceramics and other "higher" crafts. Others, like Frank Roberts, J. O. Brew, Paul Nesbitt, A. V. Kidder, Hiroshi Daifuku, and Watson Smith have contested the validity of the Mogollon concept and have seen the Mogollon and Anasazi as merely variants of the same general pattern. (Wendorf 1953:4–5)

As Wendorf (1953) pointed out, Paul Sidney Martin quickly became a Mogollon advocate and, in 1939, based on survey information from Gila Pueblo, he would embark on a fifteen-year program of excavating Mogollon sites in western New Mexico along with John B. Rinaldo. In initial opposition to the Mogollon as a separate culture were the formidable A. V. Kidder, acknowledged patriarch of southwestern archaeology, and J. O. Brew of the Peabody Museum at Harvard University, at that time the most influential institution in American archaeology (see Wendorf 2008:64). Others would join the fray at various intervals to provide their particular views of the Mogollon.

Wendorf (1953) also pointed out two of the most cogent points in the argument. One was the issue of dating—of Mogollon culture in general and of ceramics specifically—and the other was whether Mogollon as a valid entity could be extended beyond AD 1000. "One of the most critical differences of opinion between the pro- and anti-Mogollonists," he wrote, "is the relative dating of sites in the Mogollon and Anasazi areas. . . . The Mogollonists have long maintained that pottery was known in the Mogollon area considerably before it made its appearance among the Anasazi. . . . The 'Pro-Mogollonists' contend that this validates the Mogollon as a separate group" (Wendorf 1953:4–5).

The "Anti-Mogollon" group, Wendorf (1953:4–5) wrote,

> argued that the evidence for Mogollon ceramics earlier than Anasazi has not been conclusively demonstrated. They have further maintained that if ceramics were introduced from Mexico, as most Southwestern archaeologists believe, then it is to be expected that ceramic

horizons would be found in the southern part of the area which are earlier than those farther north. In addition, they state . . . that merely having ceramics early does not make them a separate cultural entity. (Smith 1949:68)

Those who supported the Mogollon concept were themselves divided into what Wendorf (1953:4–5) called two "schools." One school contended that the Mogollon were a valid and separate cultural entity only before about AD 1000, after which time the Mogollon were "submerged" in a wave of Anasazi traits that obliterated cultural differences. The second school considered the Mogollon a separate entity through the entire cultural sequence. Throughout the 1940s and 1950s, Erik K. Reed, who had worked at the Harris Village in 1934 and at Snaketown the following winter, would clarify arguments in support of the Mogollon and expand the concept to include the post–AD 1000, pueblo-building people.

Against the academic might of the Harvard crew who formed the core of the anti-Mogollonists, Haury adopted a counterstrategy based in the empirical results of survey and excavation. In 1939, he established a summer field school in the Forestdale Valley of east-central Arizona that provided evidence and tree-ring dates—one of the deficiencies in the Mogollon dating argument—for a pit-house-living Mogollon people similar to what he had found in New Mexico. After World War II, Haury moved the field school to Point of Pines, where fifteen years of research documented a further expansion of Mogollon and provided the evidence for Joe Ben Wheat's (1955) classic synthesis of Mogollon culture prior to AD 1000 that quieted the controversy, and, we think, ended it for Haury.

Having summarized the salient details of the controversy, we open our story with a bit of history, beginning in 1904 with Haury's boyhood, family, and education in Newton, Kansas—the first place in Haury's personal landscape that we visit.

2
Newton, Kansas

> A prairie never rests for long, nor does it permit anything else
> to rest. It has barriers to neither men nor wind and encour-
> ages them to run together, which may be why grasslands men
> are notorious travelers and hard-goers, driven by wind and
> running with it, wild and free.
>
> —John Madson (1982:52)

The land on which Emil Walter Haury was born and that nurtured him through childhood and young manhood is a hard land, a place where the wind cuts like a knife and has whittled down the contours of topography to the bare bones. Newton, Kansas, sits on the edge of the tallgrass prairie in the heart of America. Home to a colony of Mennonite pioneers who busted sod and built a community on hard work and turkey red wheat, Newton also was the site of Bethel College, the Mennonite institution that Haury's father helped to raise from the tall grass and where he taught. In this unique setting, a place where intellectual pursuits, a simple lifestyle, faith, and hard labor merged, nature and nurture combined to shape the person who became the famous archaeologist, the scientist and humanist, an individual with keen intellect and creative insights.

Haury was born May 2, 1904, in Newton, Kansas, to Gustav Adolf (1863–1926) and Clara Katharina Ruth (1865–1935) Haury, the youngest of four boys. Family histories in the Mennonite Library and Archives at Bethel College tell that Gustav's father, Jacob, was born in Bavaria and emigrated to the United States in 1848. Married in Iowa to Maria Schmidt, Jacob Haury moved his family to Moundridge, Kansas, where they produced eleven children, of whom Gustav was the eldest.

In the late 1800s, when many Mennonites moved to Kansas from other parts of the Midwest, Kansas had not yet become the completely humanized agrarian landscape that it is today. Prairie grasses still rippled in the wind like ocean waves, and the flat land stretched limitless and feature-less in all directions. We could not learn what Jacob Haury did for a liv-ing, but we guess that he probably farmed the rich, black Kansas soil that today yields wheat, corn, soybeans, alfalfa, and milo, as did his Mennon-ite brethren. It must have been an exhausting life. A homesteader woman quoted at the Kauffman Museum in Newton wrote, "Life was wretchedly uncomfortable. . . . We made the most of our circumstances and of each other. . . . Life was worthwhile, even then."

The Mennonite movement to Kansas in the 1870s was simply the last chapter in a long history of perpetual migration. From Holland the Men-nonites moved to Germany, and from Germany to Russia, eventually dis-covering a new life in the Americas. Historian Cornelius J. Dyck (1993:211) has written that their history "reflects an endless pilgrimage from one corner of the earth to the other." Clearly, Mennonites were fearless trav-elers, unafraid to tackle new lives in unknown lands. Mennonites value the simple life, shaping their communities around discipleship, group discipline, compassion, witnessing, suffering, and rejection of violence and war, but they also value education. The history of Mennonite migra-tions is in part a history of struggling to develop educational institutions to train ministers and their congregations. Mennonites were not per-mitted to have their own schools in Germany, for example. In Kansas, the desire to develop Mennonite centers of higher learning began with the Emmental school in 1882, which became the Halstead Mennonite Seminary the following year. A short-lived, separate department for train-ing Native American students opened at this college preparatory and teacher-training institution in 1885. Gustav Haury, who at the time was principal of the Hillsboro school, came to Halstead in 1892 and taught English there until Bethel College opened.

As Peter J. Wedel writes in *The Story of Bethel College* (1954), the 1880s were a time of transition for Mennonites. The threshing stone—a cruci-form block carved from local limestone—had been replaced by the thresh-ing machine, the ox cart by the spring wagon and buggy. Wood-frame long houses sheltering more than thirty immigrant families gave way to indi-vidual cabins and then to more spacious and better-constructed homes. A greater variety of foods replaced the spare European diet. A cultural and intellectual boom accompanied these changes in technology and life-style, and one of its outgrowths was Bethel College (fig. 2.1).

The site selected for the college "was pleasantly located about a mile north of Newton on a slight elevation that has since come to be known

Figure 2.1 The Bethel College Administration Building, dedicated in 1893, as it looks today, framed by green grass and trees. (Photograph by Jefferson Reid)

as Mt. Hebron" (Wedel 1954:55). A photograph taken of Bethel College in 1901 shows the college buildings rising from the treeless prairie. Today, the campus is the epitome of midwestern landscaping, graced by huge, old shade trees, flowerbeds, and lawns. Mt. Hebron itself is invisible to southwesterners born and bred in mountain country. Bethel College, now located in North Newton (incorporated 1938), opened its doors in 1893. The campus was a patchwork of old and new buildings (the Halstead Seminary buildings were moved to the new campus) and faculty homes. Gustav Haury was one of the founding faculty members of the pioneer college, teaching literature, Latin, and German. The 1901 photograph shows the family home that was constructed in 1898, a simple two-story building of necessity large enough to house a growing family (fig. 2.2). Records conflict, but apparently the Haury family home is no longer standing.

Although Gustav had little formal university schooling, being limited to two years at the University of Kansas, he was described as a man of

Figure 2.2 The Haury home (second from right) from the Bethel College Administration Building, with the spare landscape of Newton, Kansas, in the background. (Photograph courtesy of Loren and Jan Danson Haury)

broad interests and keen intellect. Photographs show the senior Haury to be a stern-faced, bald, and bearded academician (fig. 2.3). Gustav Haury Sr. eventually would serve as treasurer and business manager of the college and secretary of the faculty, as well as teaching classes for more than thirty years.

In this Mennonite academic community in the heart of the American Midwest, Haury and his brothers were raised in seemingly idyllic surroundings. Clara Haury was clearly an immensely proud and doting mother of four handsome young men (see fig. 2.3). We suspect it was she who had them photographed annually in coat and tie from 1909 until shortly before Irvin's tragic death of meningitis in 1918. Irvin (1892–1918) was the oldest of the boys. One wonders how the pacifist Mennonites responded to the horrors of World War I, but Irvin evidently felt the call to serve. He enlisted as a medical noncombatant and was awaiting deployment at Camp Funston when he contacted spinal meningitis. After only

Figure 2.3 The Haury family circa 1907. They are, from left to right, Alfred, Gustav Jr., Gustav Sr., Emil, Clara Katharina, and Irvin. (Photograph courtesy of Loren and Jan Danson Haury)

twelve hours' illness, he passed away. A photograph depicts his funeral cortege leaving the Bethel College main building, with college president John W. Kliewer in the lead. In an odd coincidence, many young men from Tucson also were sent to Camp Funston, which suffered one of the greatest outbreaks of Spanish influenza in the country.

Gustav Adolph Haury Jr. (1895–1952) appears to have inherited the Haury birthright to follow his father as a teacher at Bethel College. He taught English, was physical instructor for men, and was one of the most popular men on the campus. Third in line was Alfred Carl (1898–1940), who also died young. The young Emil may have been justifiably haunted by the prospects of a shortened life expectancy seemingly characteristic of the Haury men and thus encouraged to be diligent and efficient in every endeavor.

Of the experiences and influences that affected the young Haury, we know little. Unlike Jesse Jennings, whose autobiography, *Accidental Archaeologist* (1994), devotes a considerable number of pages to describing the hardships and challenges of his boyhood, Haury's own recollections are abbreviated to include only those experiences that steered him toward archaeology at an early age. Loren Haury, the younger of Emil and Hulda Haury's two sons, recalled that his father's "first and secret ambition" was to be an archaeologist (L. Haury 2004a:55). Haury himself credits early interests to reading about Indians in the *American Boy Magazine* and to a book, inspiring to him, called *Two Little Savages, Being the Adventures of Two Boys Who Lived as Indians and What They Learned* (1903, republished 1962) by Ernest Thompson Seton, naturalist to the government of Manitoba. Seton's "two little savages" are young boys intent on learning the woodcraft of the North American Indian. The book is dedicated "To WOODCRAFT by one who owes it many lasting PLEASURES." It is an idealized portrayal of Native American life and European American boyhood and is fully consonant with the masculine, naturalistic themes of the Boy Scouts of America. It also is in accord with the highly romanticized, late Victorian notion of Indians as pure and noble beings.

Other influences brought young Haury into contact with Native Americans, even in the unlikely Bethel College setting. The Newton area was the original home of the Wichita, who had been on hand to greet the puzzled soldiers of Coronado's army when they traveled to Quivira in 1541. In addition, a key Mennonite concept is service to the community, giving of oneself and through the church to fill society's needs. Mennonites sponsored orphanages, established relief funds, and contributed to scholarships. They also worked in far-flung corners of the earth as missionaries, reaching out to Native Americans in North and South America and to the peoples of India and Africa. Heinrich Richert Voth was a pillar of the college community who carried mission outreach to Arizona Territory, where he established a Mennonite mission at the Hopi village of Oraibi, Arizona, in 1893. In addition to teaching at the ill-fated Indian department at the Halstead school, Voth brought a number of Native American students to study at Bethel College.

Southwestern archaeologist Raymond H. Thompson (1995:642) wrote that "Emil learned about Arizona Indians firsthand when a young Hopi woman came to Newton to be a student at Bethel Academy, the preparatory school division of Bethel College. Polingaysi Qoyawayma (later Elizabeth Q. White) was the daughter of 'Freddie' Qoyawayma, the Hopi assistant to Heinrich Richert Voth." Thompson continued, "Housing for her was a problem, but Gustav and Clara Haury helped solve it by inviting Polingaysi to live in the Haury home."

Another event that connected Haury to Arizona and the Southwest was his parents' trip to Walnut Canyon near Flagstaff, where they picked up a piece of black-on-white pottery. Back home in Kansas, it was added to a cabinet of prized curios. In later years, Haury would recall that it was a type known today as Kayenta Black-on-white. We wonder how the Haurys felt about the strange southwestern landscape and if they conveyed their wonder to their son. Nothing could be less like the flat, cold Kansas prairie than Arizona, with its massive mountains, carved canyons, and eerily beautiful deserts. The one was marked into strongly geometric patterns by plow and combine, a land where wilderness lived only in memory. The other was little but wilderness, wild and unsettled, a true outpost of the rough-and-tumble West that would not reach statehood until 1912. In Kansas, the West's layers of vegetation and topography were chiseled raw. Madson (1982:18–19) wrote that the pioneers "stood under an infinite vault of sky in a world reduced to three immensities: the grass below, the sky above, and the single horizon beyond."

Haury graduated from Bethel Academy and completed two years at Bethel College. As a sophomore, he was a charter member of the Delta Sigma science society, secretary of the Cabinet of the YMCA, business manager for the 1925 *Graymaroon* (the Bethel College yearbook), and member of the Letter Club for intercollegiate athletics. Loren Haury (2004b:11) recalls that his father was interested in music as well as science. He played clarinet in the Bethel College orchestra, sang in the men's chorus, and toured with a quartet of friends who sang at local Kansas towns. Hulda Penner, whose family also was prominent in the Bethel College community, had caught his eye. She was a freshman at Bethel and an associate editor for the 1925 *Graymaroon*. Three years later, as soon as Haury had graduated with a master's degree, Hulda Penner would become Mrs. Emil W. Haury.

Indeed, it was family and friendship that linked Haury with the man who would make the archaeology dream come true—Byron Cummings. Emil R. Riesen was a colleague of Haury's father at Bethel College, teaching German and education. He was married to Rachel Penner, sister of Hulda Penner. In 1918, Riesen resigned his position for "a larger field of service, better remuneration, and an improved climate" (Wedel 1954:197) at the University of Arizona, where he served as registrar and taught philosophy. Haury (E. Haury 2004:55) recalled that "his [Riesen's] wife's brother was a good friend of mine, and through him I learned that Byron Cummings, head of the Department of Archaeology, made yearly expeditions into northern Arizona and southern Utah in search of cliff ruins. . . . Hearing those tantalizing stories made me dream of joining Cummings someday."

In the winter of 1923–24, Cummings traveled to Washington, D.C., to argue for support from the National Geographic Society for his work at Cuicuilco. According to Haury, Professor Riesen persuaded Cummings to stop at Bethel College on the way and lecture on his work. Haury immediately made arrangements to meet with Cummings and try to enlist on one of Cummings's famous expeditions to the Four Corners region. A series of disappointments ensued, as Cummings's work at Cuicuilco continued, and no Four Corners expeditions were forthcoming. Cummings and Haury kept in contact, however, and in March 1925, Cummings told Haury that if he was really interested in archaeology, he could learn in no better place than Mexico. This "proved to be the turning point" for the young Haury (E. Haury 2004:58). Gustav Haury Sr. offered to pay his son's way to Mexico, and Cummings in turn promised to provide board and lodging in Mexico, pay Haury's way from Mexico City to Tucson, and give him a job so that Haury could attend school at the University of Arizona! It was, Haury (2004:58) recalled, "the kind of 'break' that comes only once in a lifetime." We can only imagine the tremendous excitement and apprehension Haury must have felt facing a dream come true, a foreign country, and an eminent archaeologist with whom to work.

So that was how, in 1925, Haury "came to be on that train making the long trek through Oklahoma and Texas into Mexico" (E. Haury 2004:58). All the pieces were in place for Haury to become a member of a prominent academic family. Haurys were seemingly everywhere in Bethel College faculty and administration. In addition to his father and brother, Haury's brother Irvin's widow, Cora Molzen Haury, was instructor in history. In fact, the same day that Haury received the letter from Cummings inviting him to Cuicuilco, the high-school principal also called with an informal promise of a job. Haury left Newton, Kansas, and Bethel College in 1925 at the age of twenty-one and began what turned out to be a totally different career path from the one apparently ordained by local fates. It was a flip of the dice, an accident of history (E. Haury 2004:58). "Otherwise," he recalled, "I would probably this day be teaching high school in Kansas" (E. Haury 2004:58).

Regardless, the lessons learned in an educational environment of devoted teaching and institutional service exemplified so well by his father,

Gustav Haury Sr., must have served Haury in good stead throughout his own academic career. In February 1926, Professor Gustav A. Haury Sr. resigned his position as treasurer and business manager, asking for a leave of absence because of ill health. He had missed his first day of school in more than thirty-six years of teaching. Not long after, on June 18, 1926, the senior Haury passed away. The last of the original Bethel College faculty was gone.

Peter J. Wedel (1954:313) wrote of Gustav Haury Sr. in terms that those who were privileged to know his son would recognize: "A keen intellect, sound judgment, a strong but withal pleasing personality, firm convictions, positively but not dogmatically expressed, wide reading and intelligent observation gave him a breadth of outlook and a sympathetic attitude that made him one of the chief moulders of educational policy." Wedel further memorialized Gustav Haury in the *Graymaroon* of 1927 as "a man of exceptional soundness of judgment and clarity of vision," coupled with considerable intellect, humor, broadmindedness and tolerance, and public spirit. His philosophy was "that education should train not only the head, the hand and the eye, but the heart and conscience as well, that it should make for efficiency not only in the professions or in higher intellectual pursuits, but that it should prepare for genuine Christian service." No one could come under his instruction in the classroom, Wedel wrote, without feeling the influence of his strong personality and having his or her life enriched thereby.

By that time, the prairie was essentially gone, surviving only in patches and scraps. But the roots of the prairie past remained strong and must have shaped Haury's personality, as the land affects us all. The prairie legacy was the boundless landscape, the pioneer tradition of hard work, faith, and a necessarily primal and deep connection to land and weather. To these we add the Mennonite tradition of service, self-sacrifice, and community and the intellectual tradition of the Haury family. Thompson knew Haury as well as anyone. Summarizing the values that characterized Haury and his hometown bride, Hulda Penner, Thompson wrote:

Emil and Hulda came from a liberal Mennonite world that placed high value on education, but had no restrictions on the use of mechanical means of transportation or electricity and no mandated style of clothing. There were, of course, many of the same stern attitudes toward social behavior and the interpretation of the Bible that characterized many Protestant communities in this country in the early years of this

Figure 2.4 Emil Haury, age 21, at his first archaeological excavation, Cuicuilco, Mexico, in 1925. (Courtesy of the Arizona State Museum; neg. no. 7735)

century. Although Emil and Hulda did not remain active in the Mennonite church and abandoned many of its doctrines, they never lost those family-instilled, traditional Mennonite values of hard work and industry, integrity and honesty, cleanliness and simplicity of living, personal loyalty and commitment, and cooperation and help for others. (Thompson 1995:645)

In June of 1925, Haury left Newton, Kansas, to join Cummings's excavations at Cuicuilco on the outskirts of Mexico City, and he never returned except to visit family (fig. 2.4). Leaving Kansas, Haury left behind a landscape of wind and sky, earth and stars, a country shaped by raw wind, blazing sun, prairie fire, and bitter, drifting snow. In such a landscape, a person becomes the center of the earth, reliant only on himself or herself to make a path or risk becoming lost in the great, grassy ocean. There is no place to hide in this land of expanses. The spirit must rise to encompass the horizon, to bear the burden of storm and endure the ceaseless cutting of the wind. It was a challenge that Haury did not fail to meet.

3
Arizona

The Southwest has been from the beginning of archaeological
work there the greatest of all natural laboratories for studying
people in relationship to their physical setting. In the space
of a few hundred miles a traveler experiences sharp changes
from desertic, to mountainous, to high plateau environments—
three markedly different worlds inhabited by three sets of
people who played out a fascinating complexity of relationships.

—Emil Haury (1985b:393)

Haury was twenty-one in 1925, when he joined Cummings's expedition
at Cuicuilco on the outskirts of Mexico City. During the twelve-year
period from 1925 to 1937, he rocketed from inexperienced undergraduate
student to seasoned professional archaeologist and head of the Department of Archaeology at the University of Arizona. That this passage was
so rapid was due in part to the unusual circumstances of his appren-
ticeship under three remarkably different, intellectually energetic men he
encountered in Arizona—Cummings, A. E. Douglass, and Harold S. Gladwin. Their sequence of association with Haury was as significant to his
professional development as was the particular contribution of each man.

The wandering path that led Haury to Arizona began with a dawn
departure and a great deal of anticipation. "June 11, 1925—4:55 a.m. this
morning should mark the beginning of a new and novel experience." So
he wrote (E. Haury 2004:59) of his leaving Newton on the no. 17 train for
the long trip by rail to Mexico City. Its extended misery (Haury's own
term) no doubt meant that Cummings's appearance at the train station
to greet Haury was a most welcome sight. As published, Haury's abbreviated Cuicuilco diary (E. Haury 2004) catalogs more than a young man's
naive astonishment at being immersed in a foreign culture. It also reveals glimpses of the personality of the man who would become Haury's

mentor. Haury wrote of Cummings's kindness in trying to teach him Spanish and of his futile attempt to trick Cummings with green glass in place of obsidian. Haury also recorded Cummings's fury at the antics of their hostess's pet raven, Aquervo. "Dean C. is on his trail, and there will be a sick raven if he gets him" (E. Haury 2004:67). More importantly, we learn of Cummings's confidence in leaving Haury in charge of the laborers, his interest in amassing collections for the University of Arizona, and his cooking skills.

In his personal recollections, Haury recalled his sense of wonderment at Cuicuilco's monumental architecture. His words provide insight into Haury's understanding of human endeavors past and present and the inimitable forces of the environment in shaping them. On his first day, he stood in disbelief "looking at a monumental building about 400 feet in diameter and over 70 feet high, trying to understand the cataclysmic event of nature that sent down from the mountains a lava flow locking and partially burying the structure in a vise-like grip, marveling at the fervor which impelled the builders to erect it, and admiring the archaeologists' boldness and courage to uncover and understand it" (Haury 1979:7).

On September 9, Haury left Mexico City, and he arrived in Tucson at 6:00 a.m. on September 12. So ended eight weeks "of profitable and valuable experience" (E. Haury 2004:82). It was the beginning of a lifelong immersion in the archaeology of the American Southwest and a distinguished career at the University of Arizona.

Tucson

Haury transferred to the Department of Archaeology at the University of Arizona, where he completed his junior and senior years, his master's degree in 1928, and where, during the 1928–29 academic year, he held his first teaching position. By 1925, Haury already had experienced the plains of Kansas, the highlands of central Mexico, and had been introduced to the expanses of the Sonoran Desert. Shortly, he would add the rugged uplands of central Arizona and the pine forests of New Mexico to his geographic experience. It is hard for us to imagine, inured as we are to the sprawl of housing developments, strip malls, golf courses, and high-end resorts that constitutes today's Tucson, what the city must have looked like to Haury in 1925. The university had yet to create the enormous web of brick buildings, dormitories, parking garages, and athletic fields that characterizes it now. But the striking desert landscape surely was much the same.

Tucson lies in a basin encircled by mountains, the characteristic features that give the basin-and-range physiographic province its label. The "sky islands" of the Catalina and Rincon mountains rise thousands of feet to the north and east. The Tucson Mountains, jagged remnants of an ancient volcanic caldera, separate Tucson from the traditional desert lands of the Tohono O'odham peoples to the west. Through the basin winds the dry bed of the Santa Cruz River, which in ancient times and even in the nineteenth century had permanent surface flow. The land is rocky and sandy, the vegetation is prickly, and more than anything, the desert is hot. Eight weeks at Cuicuilco may have preconditioned Haury to expect the unexpected, but the Tucson desert, with its peculiarly anthropomorphic cactus and its mountains carved like a movie-scenery backdrop against a flawless western sky, was as different from Kansas as any place could be.

Archaeologists have chronicled the history of the Department of Anthropology (Thompson 2005) and the Arizona State Museum (Wilcox 2005), but their words fail to give a sense of how thoroughly both were the creation of Cummings (see Fowler 2000). The University of Arizona was founded in 1885. Built on forty acres of land not far east of downtown Tucson, it opened its doors to students in 1891, when a single building, today's Old Main, housed faculty, classrooms, library, and students. The Arizona State Museum was established in 1893, when it was called the Territorial Museum. Originally, it also was housed in Old Main. Cummings had come to Arizona in 1915 from the University of Utah, where a confrontation of politics and religion ended his twenty-two years of service there (Bostwick 2006; Fowler 2000; Thompson 2005).

Cummings's position was professor of archaeology and director of the Arizona State Museum, an inactive and motley collection of birds, eggs, nests, minerals, some ethnological material, and a few Indian artifacts when he arrived (Thompson 2005; Wilcox 2005). From 1925 until 1929, the museum and the archaeology department were located in the Agriculture Building (now the Forbes Building). Cummings quickly refashioned the museum, developed the Department of Archaeology into a recognized research and teaching center, and created the first archaeological field schools at the university. Under his tutelage grew "a strong and devoted group of students who were destined to become anthropological luminaries in their own right" (Thompson 2005:331). One of these students was Haury. He would assume Cummings's mantle and carve the department into his own likeness.

Although the university had grown, Tucson still retained something of a Wild West aura in 1925. Arizona had been a state only thirteen years, after all. Historian C. L. Sonnichsen (1982) has characterized the 1920s, when Haury arrived, as Tucson's "gold-plated" decade. The town was approaching a population of 35,000, and enrollment at the University of Arizona exceeded 1,000 students for the first time in 1920. The stately, Arizona mission-style El Conquistador Hotel and Isabella Greenway's Arizona Inn would soon open their doors to wealthy sun-seekers, and the predecessor of American Airlines would begin air service through Tucson in 1928. Nevertheless, the dude-ranch industry remained one of Arizona's economic mainstays, and Tucson still drowsed under the sizzling summer sun.

Haury (1979) recalled that his experience in Mexico with Cummings had given him entree into the Cummings family, which was in some ways as important as his professional relationship with "the Dean" (Cummings's affectionate nickname). Haury was a frequent visitor at the Cummings home, helping to do chores, run errands, and even teach Mrs. Cummings to drive the family Ford, which Haury recalled as a harrowing experience. At the university, Haury was also Cummings's right-hand man, research assistant, and chauffeur. Cummings had grown in stature at the university, serving as dean of the College of Letters, Arts, and Sciences; dean of men; and president (Wilcox 2005). Between 1927 and 1928, Cummings served as the ninth president of the university. As Cummings's chauffeur, Haury was introduced to prominent politicians throughout Arizona. He was among the privileged few students in attendance at the first Pecos Conference that Kidder convened. It was a rather informal gathering of archaeologists and ethnographers held at Kidder's field camp at Pecos, New Mexico, and hosted the eminent scholars of the day (Woodbury 1993). Although there was a full agenda for the meeting, the lasting result was codification of the Pecos classification for the prehistoric Basketmaker-Pueblo cultural sequence—Basketmaker II and III, Pueblo I, II, III, IV, and Pueblo V, or historical pueblo. The first Pecos Conference was a landmark defining the major temporal and cultural units for the American Southwest.

Cummings, who was an indefatigable explorer, frequently took students to the field on weekends and holidays. It was on one of these trips in response to a call from a teacher at the Double Adobe school near Douglas, Arizona, that Haury had his first brush with a major archaeological discovery—the association of human-made tools with an extinct form of elephant. Cummings did not promote the 1926 Double Adobe find, and it was soon overshadowed by the discovery that same year of similar associations at Folsom, New Mexico (Meltzer 2006; Thompson 1983). We have suspected that Cummings's reticence in promoting the Double Adobe finds was colored by the equally controversial claim for an eighth-century Roman-Jewish settlement on the west bank of the Santa Cruz River outside of Tucson (Burgess 2009). The controversy over the "Silverbell Lead Crosses"—crosses, swords, and other lead artifacts inscribed with schoolbook Latin and Hebrew characters found along Silverbell Road and claimed to date to the eighth century AD—would expose Haury to the ambiguities of the archaeological record and the power of belief over empirical evidence. Haury actually inspected one of the finds, supposedly in situ, and concluded that it had been planted, which, along with other evidence for recent manufacture, allowed the university in late 1929 to exercise the escape clause in its contract to purchase the artifacts for $16,000.

Cummings also was responsible for Haury's first exposure to the archaeology of northeastern Arizona. In 1927, Cummings directed Haury to collect Basketmaker material for the museum's collection. For most of the summer, Haury worked in the area, collecting artifacts and fossils, acutely aware that this experience kept him apart from his future bride, who was visiting relatives in Tucson. The same year, his painstaking work extracting fossils from matrix for a geology research paper was rewarded with a trip to the Grand Canyon with a geology professor. In 1928, the newly married Haury was field foreman for excavations at Turkey Hill Pueblo, a Sinagua site near Flagstaff. The Haurys explored the ruins of Tsegi Canyon, the movie-set scenery of Monument Valley, and visited Rainbow Bridge. Haury recalled that these experiences helped a great deal several years later, when Gila Pueblo Archaeological Foundation assigned him to work at the Tusayan Ruin on the South Rim of the Grand Canyon.

In the fall of 1928, Haury began teaching at the university. He taught introductory archaeology and archaeology of the Southwest. He recalled that his inexperience led him to finish an entire semester's outline for the former course in the first lecture hour. From Cummings, a classics scholar and Victorian moralist, he had learned much. But Cummings employed an antiquarian approach to archaeological record keeping and inference with which Haury became increasingly uncomfortable. This uneasiness with Cummings's "science" and the awkwardness of that first year's teaching experience prompted Haury to look elsewhere for additional archaeological training and experience. Even so, his archaeological perspective was given its initial shape through the humanistic approach and humanitarian concern of the dynamic Cummings.

In 1929, Haury found the new experience he sought with Andrew Ellicott Douglass, the astronomer and father of dendrochronology, who would become the second major influence on Haury's scholarship (fig. 3.1). At that time, Douglass was organizing the National Geographic Society's Third Beam Expedition, and as members of that expedition team, Haury and Lyndon Hargrave supervised the unearthing of a tree-ring sample in Show Low, Arizona, on June 22, 1929. This specimen proved to bridge the apparent gap between Douglass's prehistoric and historical-period tree-ring chronologies and permitted the first accurate dating of the Southwest's major pueblo ruins. In Haury's own words, this was the most dramatic event of his archaeological career, and we cannot improve on his account of that moment (Haury 1962).

Figure 3.1 Andrew Ellicott Douglass, astronomer and father of tree-ring dating, in front of a chart of the culture sequence in the Forestdale Valley compared to the Basketmaker-Pueblo sequence of the Pecos classification. (Photograph by Emil Haury; courtesy of the Arizona State Museum; neg. no. 660)

"Finally, the answer came; and here I must quote from memory," wrote Haury (in Reid and Doyel 1986:59–60), recalling Douglass's words:

"I think we have it. Ring patterns between 1240 and 1300 of the historic sequence correspond in all important respects to the patterns in the youngest part of the prehistoric sequence. This means that there was no gap at all. The overlap of the two chronologies was only 26 years and there was no possible way to join the two on the evidence we had. Beam HH-39 has established the bridge." This was a moment of great truth, and at times like this, the truth sinks in slowly. No one spoke. Douglass was busy making mental calculations, correcting his relative dates for ruins to the years of the Christian calendar. He broke the silence in his gentle way and told the spellbound archaeologists: "This means that Pueblo Bonito was occupied in the 11th and early 12th centuries and the other large ruins of Chaco Canyon were of the same age. The ruins of Mesa Verde, Betatakin and Keet Seel are a little younger, mid-13th century."

He continued his recitation, revealing his phenomenal memory, by listing all the major sites from which he obtained wood for developing the prehistoric sequence, and delivering at the same time, a totally new and vital short course in Southwest prehistory:

For the three of us, the experience was unforgettable. To be present at the instant of the celebrated break-through in science that set the chronological house in order for the Southwestern United States was reward enough. But beyond that, was the privilege to work for a time at the side of Douglass, the scholar, the astronomer turned archaeologist.

Haury's subsequent year working with Douglass had a deep impact on his later archaeological research. Of immediate relevance were the contrasting approaches of Cummings and Douglass. Whereas Cummings observed broadly with an eye toward general humanistic implications, Douglass attended to minute detail in a precise scientific fashion. Douglass's example was not lost on young Haury, who quickly absorbed the scientific method but ultimately decided that the microscopic investigation of tree rings was not to be the major subject of his research career. Haury would, however, continue to play a prominent administrative role in the development of tree-ring research at the University of Arizona.

Working with Douglass on the nascent science of dendrochronology gave Haury a thorough appreciation for the value of its archaeological applications as well as for the importance of chronological concerns to all of prehistory. Early in his own career and before these new techniques were widely available or understood, he had demonstrated a sophisticated grasp of chronometric method and the inestimable value of pieces of burned wood for resolving questions of chronology and past behavior. The importance of dating prehistoric events and especially of establishing archaeological chronologies pervaded all of Haury's research and imbued his reconstructions of the past with lasting scientific usefulness. A large measure of this attention to chronometry must be attributed to the experiences gained by working with Douglass.

After his work with Douglass came the experience that would shape Haury's career, define the Mogollon culture, and instigate the Mogollon controversy. This was Haury's employment at Gila Pueblo Archaeological Foundation.

Globe

Harold Sterling Gladwin was a financier who fell in love with the Southwest and its prehistoric past. In 1928, with Winifred MacCurdy, who later became his wife, he established the Gila Pueblo Archaeological Foundation in Globe, Arizona. Under Gladwin's direction, Gila Pueblo's archaeological research became the most innovative and productive of the Depression era. The archaeologists of Gila Pueblo participated in exciting research and set an enviable publication record that rivaled many later developments in the field. They defined the Hohokam, Cochise, Salado, and of course, the Mogollon culture.

Gila Pueblo was built on the ruins of a prehistoric site in the romantically named Sixshooter Canyon. Like so many places in Arizona, Globe and its sister city Miami were mining towns built on the copper industry, a fact difficult to escape where the denuded tailings rise as a backdrop to the rough-and-tumble town. Globe sits on the edge of Arizona's rugged Transition Zone, where the Sonoran Desert gives way to mountainous and forested land. Higher and therefore cooler than Tucson, Globe is nevertheless firmly in the desert's grip, seriously affecting Mrs. MacCurdy's efforts to grow irises.

Gladwin spent the first winter after he purchased the site in a tent camp. Gladwin recalled that "At night it often seemed to me that I could hear the drums and the chanting of the old timers and by spring I began to feel that I had been accepted as a member of the old pueblo" (quoted in Haury 1988:8). Perhaps it was this romantic notion that inspired Gladwin to build Gila Pueblo in the style of an ancient pueblo, with plastered-adobe walls and beamed ceilings. As the prehistoric rooms were excavated, Mexican and O'odham (Pima) laborers rebuilt them. Gladwin observed that it was a relief when Mrs. MacCurdy took over the rebuilding effort, although the plan to build in the footprint of the old pueblo was abandoned with regret due to its incompatibility with modern life. When it came to the interior furnishings, the Gladwins also broke away from the pueblo style. The great Council Hall was made comfortable with an enormous rock fireplace, Arts and Crafts furniture, wrought-iron chandeliers, original oil paintings, and "one of the largest double-faced Navajo rugs ever made" (Haury 1988:20). Gila Pueblo would be Haury's home and the epicenter of his research for some time.

Haury and Gladwin had become acquainted in the winter of 1929–30, when Haury was spending hours each day peering at tree-ring specimens under a microscope. He also assisted Douglass in teaching a course on dendrochronology at the University of Arizona. Gladwin, Winifred Mac-Curdy, and Edith Sangster—the Gila Pueblo secretary—drove to Tucson from Globe to attend a number of the classes. Each man must have seen something in the other, for Gladwin extended an offer to become assistant director of Gila Pueblo, and Haury accepted.

A number of job opportunities were available to Haury in 1930. Douglass had invited him to stay on another year, Cummings requested another year of teaching, and the National Museum in Washington, D.C., offered him a position. Haury knew he was fortunate to have such choices on the threshold of the Great Depression. But he also knew he did not want a life of tree-ring analysis, and Haury confessed that he was apprehensive about moving to Washington and leaving the Southwest. But Gila Pueblo—that was an alluring possibility, dense with promise. Gladwin's offer held the prospect of ample fieldwork and publication opportunities and, equally important, support for doctoral studies. Gladwin agreed to provide time off from regular duties with financial support to pursue a PhD, if Haury would agree to stay at Gila Pueblo for three years after earning his degree. The other options could not match these advantages. The resilient young Haury would translate the frenetic schedule of fieldwork and publication, guided and supported by Gladwin's intellect, iconoclasm, and personal fortune, into significant archaeological research.

The Early Years at Gila Pueblo

Almost from the moment he arrived, Haury was thrown into the hectic activity that characterized Gila Pueblo. In June 1930, the Haurys left Tucson to join the Gila Pueblo force camped near the Tusayan Ruin on the South Rim of the Grand Canyon (fig. 3.2). It was a long day's drive in a small Chevrolet pickup truck, from Tucson to Globe, then through the Tonto Basin, the Verde Valley, and the incomparable Oak Creek Canyon over what was then a barely passable road. Interstate 17 and Arizona State Route 89A would not be constructed for decades. Haury (1979) recalled that excavations at the Tusayan Ruin alternated with harrowing surveys into the depths of the Grand Canyon. Gladwin had chosen the Grand Canyon region in part to determine whether the tremendous chasm had precluded the free exchange of information and cultural traditions from

Figure 3.2 The Gila Pueblo Archaeological Foundation staff in 1930. Seated, left to right, are Harold S. Gladwin, Winifred Jones MacCurdy (Gladwin), Nora MacCurdy, Hulda Haury, Emil Haury, and Russell Hastings. Behind them, left to right, are Edith Sangster, Evelyn Dennis, and George Dennis. (Courtesy of the Arizona State Museum; neg. no. 72734)

north to south. Haury's report on the kivas of the Tusayan Ruin underscored his nascent ability to grasp the subtle distinctions of ancient settlements located on the boundaries of cultural groups. He observed that the Tusayan Ruin was situated on the periphery of the Kayenta Anasazi area and explained the unusual carelessness of construction in the kivas as the probable consequence of being removed from the center of cultural development.

Shortly thereafter, Gladwin proposed an expedition to the cliff ruins of the Sierra Ancha (Spanish for "wide mountains"), now a wilderness area in the uplands of central Arizona. Two weeks in the saddle convinced Haury of the necessity to meld the practical with one's research goals if success were to be achieved. Next followed a brief stint at Rye Creek Ruin north of Globe, an exercise Gladwin closed down unexpectedly and without explanation.

Two events of early 1931 played a central role in establishing a framework for discovery of the Mogollon. The first event was the excavation of Roosevelt 9:6, a Hohokam pit-structure village located on the south bank of the Salt River at Roosevelt Lake. This site would define the Hohokam Colonial period. The second event was the Gila Pueblo Conference, Gladwin's attempt to standardize archaeological taxonomy beyond the limited scope of the 1927 Pecos Conference.

Roosevelt 9:6

The receding water of Roosevelt Lake in the Tonto Basin of central Arizona had exposed cremations and pottery of the Red-on-Buff culture, which at that time was the label for the Hohokam. This cultural group was Gladwin's obsession and the research focus of Gila Pueblo's fieldwork. In 1927, Gladwin had excavated at Casa Grande National Monument while working for the Southwest Museum in Los Angeles. He had uncovered stratigraphic evidence for the superpositioning and temporal sequencing of two different cultures represented by distinctive pottery types—red painted on a buff background and polychrome painted in black and white on a red slip. Gladwin had engaged the Gila Pueblo staff in extensive archaeological survey to trace the extent of the Red-on-Buff culture. The site on the lake was labeled Roosevelt 9:6 in the Gila Pueblo nomenclature, and it gave every indication of dating to the early end of Gladwin's red-on-buff pottery sequence. Under Haury's direction, excavation began at Roosevelt 9:6 in mid-January 1931 and ended a few weeks later.

The site was a hamlet of fourteen pit structures, all excavated or tested and believed to represent the total number of dwellings. The archaeologists discovered two cremation cemeteries, two shallow refuse mounds, and a large rock-filled pit-oven, or roasting pit. The red-on-buff pottery placed the site slightly earlier than the Grewe site near Coolidge, Arizona (Arthur Woodward of the Los Angeles Museum of History, Science, and Art had excavated there and published a report in 1931), and solidly within what Haury's site report would elaborate as the Colonial period of the Hohokam culture.

The Roosevelt 9:6 report appeared in early 1932 as Medallion Paper 11 and was the first publication to use the Hohokam label for a prehistoric site. More important to our story, however, is that Roosevelt 9:6 provided Haury with firsthand knowledge and direct contact with the archaeological remains of the Hohokam culture during the Pueblo I period (AD 700–900) of the Pecos classification. Haury was able to conclude the Roosevelt 9:6 report with a list of contrasting traits comparing the Hohokam and the Basketmaker-Pueblo at a time before AD 1000, and he would have this trait list in the back of his mind during his mountain survey of 1931 when the first traces of the Mogollon would be discovered.

We also suspect Haury's work in the environs of Roosevelt Lake made him acutely aware of the intimate connection between land and culture, which he would pursue in subsequent studies of the Hohokam in the Gila River valley and the Papaguería, the desert homeland of the Tohono O'odham (formerly known as the Papago) west of Tucson. Living and working at Gila Pueblo, which Haury (1988:15) described as "entirely in keeping with the environment" surely had a similar effect. Whereas lives on the Kansas plains were shaped by sky, storm, and relentless wind, in the desert, it was the ceaseless quest for water that drove the human experience and molded the homes and canals fashioned from the desert soil itself.

Gila Pueblo Conference

A mere four years after its adoption, some archaeologists had become dissatisfied with the Pecos classification developed at the 1927 Pecos Conference. Harold S. Colton had founded the Museum of Northern Arizona the same year that Gila Pueblo was established, and he had been investigating the ruins of the Sinagua (Spanish for "without water") who had lived in the Flagstaff area and the northern Verde Valley. According to Haury (1988:41), "the differences growing in the minds of Gladwin and Colton about the systems of classifying cultures, the naming of temporal stages, and the treatment of pottery as a way of recognizing cultural change, led to the notion of a conference." The conference so invented was held at Gila Pueblo on April 16–18, 1931, with twenty-six attendees representing eight southwestern institutions in Arizona, New Mexico, and southern California. We again turn to Haury (1988:42–43), who wrote that

> the purpose of the conference was to attempt to solve the various problems of nomenclature and classification which, in field work done by these institutions, have become acute since the Pecos Conference of 1927. In the matter of the Pecos classification, it is recognized that the epochal stages implied by the Pecos classification are, in general, fundamental to the evolution of the Basket Maker and Pueblo cultures. It is believed, however, that the use of a numerical sequence has resulted in: the establishment of definite horizons and the implementation of a time element through the use of a comparative terminology, which are not appropriate to the entire area; the implication of cultural homogeneity in all areas, which does not exist; a rigidity of classification, whereas field work which has been done since its formulation has shown that the utmost elasticity is needed. On the basis of the above limitations we believe that a present classification should be based on intra-cultural rather than inter-cultural distinctions, pending the accumulation of sufficient data to establish correlation. (Haury 1988:42–43)

Haury went on to write that "confusion has been created by the careless use of terms in designating peoples, cultures and geographical areas" (Haury 1988:43).

The Gila Pueblo Conference was significant to the Mogollon discovery in that it raised the issue of the Pecos classification's inadequacy and firmly established the taxonomic reality of a Hohokam people different from the Basketmaker-Pueblo. Haury, as a participant in the conference—perhaps the youngest, for he was two weeks away from turning twenty-seven—was fully attuned to the taxonomic problems facing southwestern archaeologists at that time.

A few years after joining Gila Pueblo, the Haurys moved into the refurbished house in which the Healey family, original owners of Gila Pueblo, had lived. Mrs. Healey's "museum"—a ghoulish exhibit of gilded and crochet-covered pots, skulls outfitted with marble eyes atop mannequins dressed in Army jackets, and boot-shaped pots labeled as prehistoric bedpans—became Haury's study. As he noted (Haury 1979), the gilded pots and human skeletons were long gone. Gila Pueblo meant serious archaeological business, and Haury was shortly to embark on an archaeological journey that in one way or another would consume his professional life.

Prelude to the Summer of Discovery

If we discount the ubiquitous shadow of chance, few archaeologists have been better prepared than Haury to see a pattern that others before him had failed to notice. He was raised in an academic home where intellectual pursuits were the family business. He was privileged to be associated with mentors the likes of which are seldom equaled. Haury (1988:59) acknowledged the importance of his mentors when he wrote:

> [Gladwin's] mental energy and breadth of outlook, whatever one might think of his eventual reconstructions, were mind-boggling to a novice like me. As I think back to the principal characters who materially shaped my career and assess their various influences, they appear to me as follows: from Cummings I gained much in humanism; from A. E. Douglass, the discipline of a scientist; from Colton, discipline and the interrelatedness of the branches of science; from Kidder, a rigorous attention to detail, the melding of systematics, the necessity not to lose sight of the human factor in the process, and the desirability of using a form of rhetoric comprehensible to all; from Tozzer at Harvard, the importance of the learning process through teaching; and from Gladwin, the creativity, imagination, and the courage to depart from the accepted model. In his view, straying from the well-trodden path was the way advances were to be made, for better or worse. (Haury 1988:59)

The energy and optimism of youth also was a contributing factor. At that time, Haury was only twenty-seven, the same age when Reid first worked in the Arizona mountains, and we suspect that Haury's motivation in the summer of 1931 centered in part on the joys of looking for prehistoric sites and camping in the forested, high country of Arizona and New Mexico before beginning graduate work in dreary Harvard classrooms in the fall. It turned out to be a summer of discovery.

4
Discovering the Mountain Mogollon

Increasing attention to those other areas, the arid desert to the
southwest and the verdant mountains to the south and east,
was being given by the staff members of newly founded
private institutions devoted to archaeology.... Their findings
quickly reinforced the beliefs that the records of the past in
the mountainous and desertic regions did not fit the Plateau
mold as outlined at Pecos.

—Emil Haury (1985a:xv)

Haury and Russell Hastings, another Gila Pueblo archaeologist, set out in
the summer of 1931 to survey the mountains of Arizona and New Mexico. The survey began as just another piece of Gladwin's master plan to
define the geographical boundaries of the Red-on-Buff culture, which
only that year had been renamed the Hohokam. The two young surveyors set out to define the eastern range of the Hohokam culture, yet they
accomplished far more in discovering evidence for the existence of previously unknown, ancient peoples whose archaeological remains would
shortly be named the Mogollon culture of Arizona and New Mexico.

On May 23, 1990, nearly sixty years after this survey of discovery,
we talked to Haury about that remarkable summer long ago. Because
the interview was taped, Haury's own words formed the framework for
understanding that event. Years later, as we began piecing together the
Mogollon story, contradictions arose concerning this survey, so we decided we needed to retrace major portions of the route. Like Stephen
Ambrose's (1996) tracing of the path taken by Lewis and Clark, our initial journey raised more questions than it answered. But it also provided
insights into the original explorers, Haury and Hastings. They were much
younger and far hardier than we, a conclusion reached over a chilled Dos
Equis Amber in the bar at Glenwood, New Mexico, after a long, hot day

of searching for the critical pit-house village called Mogollon 1:15 in the Gila Pueblo system. In June 1931, Haury had just turned twenty-seven, and in May 2000, Reid was more than twice that age.

Thankfully, answers to our questions lay in paperwork rather than in further fieldwork. An undergraduate working in the Arizona State Museum archives, Erin O'Meara, decided to take on this project for her honors thesis. She went through the Gila Pueblo survey files to pinpoint the actual date that Haury and Hastings were at specific sites and from these plot their route on maps showing the roads of the period. To our surprise, O'Meara demonstrated that Haury's sixty-year-old recollection of the 1931 survey had merged two separate expeditions. One took place in the fall of 1930 and traveled through Payson to Heber; the second was the 1931 summer survey. Except for the exact road from Show Low to Springerville, we now have an accurate map of their trail of discovery, which we recreate here (fig. 4.1).

The Survey of Discovery

The excursion began at Gila Pueblo on the outskirts of Globe on June 12, 1931. Haury and Hastings, who had joined the Gila Pueblo staff the previous summer, packed an old woody station wagon with camping gear and supplies. In those bygone days, archaeological reconnaissance, especially of areas as vast as those encompassed by Gila Pueblo's surveys, typically was carried out by automobile. Haury and Hastings headed east toward the Apache town of San Carlos, then north through the San Carlos Reservation over roads that still challenge the modern off-road vehicle. They crossed the Black River and drove through the Fort Apache Reservation to the town of Whiteriver, the headquarters of the White Mountain Apache Tribe. Haury and Hastings set up camp north of town. Haury recalled that their camp latrine had a stunning view of the whitewater roiling some two hundred feet below and the timber-clad slopes of Mt. Baldy, sacred to the White Mountain Apache. From there, they visited sites up the East Fork of the White River and saw pueblos that would later feature prominently in the story of the Mogollon Pueblo.

Since leaving Globe, Haury and Hastings had been traveling through a country of unparalleled ruggedness and scenic beauty. To many, visions of the Southwest comprise vistas of mesa tops, sheer sandstone cliffs, and the carved pinnacles of the Colorado Plateau. To our minds, "Southwest" means the landscape of the San Carlos and Fort Apache Reservations.

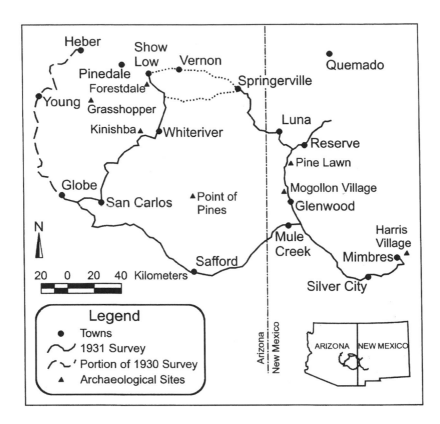

Figure 4.1 The 1931 route of the Mogollon survey of discovery, with additional places that played an important role in the Mogollon controversy. (Drawing by Brandon Gabler)

Lying below the Mogollon Rim, the geographic feature that separates the mountain Transition Zone from the Colorado Plateau, this region of Arizona is characterized by precipitous ranges, red sandstone cliffs, deep canyons, and a green canopy of juniper, piñon, oak, and ponderosa pine. Today, it is a lonely country, with few paved roads and none of the sprawling communities with their upscale malls and artificial lakes that spread across the warmer regions of the state. When Haury and Hastings were there in 1931, it must have seemed like the ends of the earth.

Not far from Whiteriver was the pueblo ruin of Kinishba ("Brown House" in the Apache language), which Haury saw for the first time on this trip (Welch 2007). The ruin was still in relatively pristine condition, having suffered little more than the occasional boredom-induced assault by soldiers from nearby Fort Apache. Cummings would not begin his excavation and restoration program there until later in the month. Haury saw a pueblo ruin of two large mounds on either side of a deep arroyo and smaller, masonry room blocks scattered around the periphery. The surface was covered with a dazzling array of painted pottery. The pueblo ruin at Cedar Creek, one-fourth the size of Kinishba and dating from the same time, sat atop a ridge overlooking the creek and commanded a sweeping view of the surrounding countryside.

Haury and Hastings ventured westward to see the fourteenth-century pueblo ruins at G Wash, Cibecue, and all the way to Grasshopper Pueblo, an ancient village whose archaeology we know well. Grasshopper is located at the far west end of the Fort Apache Reservation. Haury probably saw it much as Walter Hough did in the early 1900s, when he mapped the ruin and excavated several rooms. As at Kinishba, rubble mounds in a small meadow on either side of the shallow Salt River Draw marked the two halves of the main pueblo, and smaller room blocks were scattered around the edge and on low hills. Grasshopper was only about eight miles away from Canyon Creek Pueblo, the cliff dwelling Haury would excavate the following summer, but thirty-two years distant from the hordes of archaeologists who would come to roam the Grasshopper Plateau for three decades (Reid and Whittlesey 2005).

While they were camped north of Whiteriver, an anthropology student from Columbia University studying with famed anthropologist Franz Boas, Henrietta Schmerler, was killed in Whiteriver. The accounts of this tragic incident vary (*Time*, August 3, 1931; March 28, 1932), but they all involve the home brew called *tulapai*, a dance, and a young woman who seemingly was too naïve to be conducting ethnographic studies alone on the reservation. The following year, an Apache named Golney Seymour would be convicted of Schmerler's murder and sentenced to life imprisonment. Haury recalled the incident as most unsettling and a good reason to carry the survey farther north.

Haury and Hastings made their next camp at Show Low—"the town named by the turn of a card." It was a familiar place to Haury. As we have seen, two years earlier, in June 1929, he had helped uncover the piece of charred roof beam that completed Douglass's tree-ring chronology and made this dating technique applicable to Southwest prehistory. From Show Low, Haury and Hastings surveyed around Pinedale, Linden,

Snowflake, and Taylor. They visited the Four Mile Ruin and the sites in the Forestdale Valley.

Forestdale is a charming valley drained by Forestdale Creek and dotted with springs along the margin (fig. 4.2). At 6,500 feet above sea level, it is surrounded by ridges covered with dense stands of ponderosa pines where the earliest and latest prehistoric villagers settled. The Bluff Village, later determined to be the earliest settlement in the valley, lay atop the highest ridge, and the later Bear Village and Tla Kii Pueblo were located on the valley floor. The late thirteenth-century Forestdale Pueblo and the large fourteenth-century Tundastusa Pueblo are situated on low hills along the valley edge.

At Forestdale, Haury and Hastings found a perplexing array of sites ranging from pit-structure villages with plain brown ware pottery, to small pueblos with black-on-white pottery, to the large, late Tundastusa Pueblo with its polychrome painted pottery. All of this architectural and ceramic variability was in a small mountain valley immediately below the Mogollon Rim, adjacent to the Colorado Plateau home of the Basketmasker-Pueblo Culture defined in the Pecos classification. Forestdale raised the first questions concerning the meaning of pit-structure

Figure 4.2 A view of Forestdale Valley from Bluff Village. (Photograph by Jefferson Reid)

villages with predominately plain, brown pottery situated so near the region of pit-structure villages dominated by black-on-white and gray, plain pottery. Forestdale would later play an important, even pivotal, role in the aftermath of discovery, when Haury returned in 1939 to establish his first summer field school there.

Next, Haury and Hastings returned to Show Low and drove east to Springerville either by Vernon or through McNary; the record is unclear. From Springerville, they traveled through Luna, New Mexico, to the Pine Lawn Valley west of Reserve. Surveying around the Pine Lawn Valley, Reserve, and Apache Creek, they discovered a region teeming with pit-structure village sites covered in plain, brown pottery. Beginning in 1939, the Pine Lawn Valley would become the epicenter of Mogollon research under the direction of Paul Sidney Martin and John Rinaldo. They established a field station in the valley to serve as headquarters for the Chicago Field Museum's Southwest Expedition. Today, nothing survives of that camp or the store at Pine Lawn, other than the scant archaeological remains of early archaeologists.

Haury recalled that Gladwin and Edith Sangster joined them at Pine Lawn. He remembered this vividly because of an incident etched in his memory. Gladwin had brought along Paddy, Mrs. MacCurdy's cocker spaniel, on this trip. As the dog was romping through the bushes, a rattlesnake bit him on the muzzle. What stuck in Haury's mind was the image of Gladwin applying mouth-to-mouth suction to his fiancée's dog.

The dog saved, Haury and Hastings broke camp and traveled south along U.S. Highway 180. Near Alma, they visited Mogollon 1:15, located on a high ridge above the San Francisco River (fig. 4.3). Haury would return to this vitally important site, later named Mogollon Village, and excavate there in the summer of 1933. Along with the Harris Village, Mogollon Village would provide the fundamental data to construct the notion of the Mogollon culture.

Continuing south through Buckhorn and Silver City to the Mimbres Valley, the surveyors set up camp beside a service station, where Gladwin, Sangster, and Hulda Haury joined them. After dinner and a movie in Silver City, they returned to camp to find that they had been robbed of jewelry, a typewriter, and, most disturbing, Gladwin's revolver and ammunition. They broke camp immediately and returned to Silver City. Although their survey of the Mimbres Valley was brief, Haury also visited a pit-house-village site owned by Mrs. Harris, the Mimbres postmistress. Haury would return in the summer of 1934 to excavate the Harris Village.

Figure 4.3 The location of Mogollon Village on the ridge overlooking the San Francisco River. (Photograph by Emil Haury; courtesy of the Arizona State Museum)

Weary after a summer of camping and surveying, Haury and Hastings returned to Globe by way of Mule Creek and Safford. They had visited, recorded, and collected pottery from about three hundred archaeological sites. Back at Gila Pueblo, Sangster attached representative sherds from each site to a board for study and discussion by the staff. The Gila Pueblo sherd boards would become legendary in the annals of southwestern archaeology.

This cursory review of the trail of discovery gives little sense of what actually was a quite remarkable event—the recognition of a cultural pattern than had gone incognito until that summer and that in a few years would be presented to the archaeological community as the report of excavations at the Harris and Mogollon sites. When asked almost sixty years later what led him to recognize the Mogollon culture in scattered surface artifacts and features, Haury said:

> Remember, we had been at Show Low and to the Forestdale Valley where we found a plain ware site and adjacent to it a Pueblo I site with black-on-white pottery. And there was Tundastusa; Tundastusa had

all the polychromes. We went up on the Bluff site and found just a mere handful of pottery. Now this was adjacent to the country that produced black-on-whites. Well, that, I remember, raised some questions in our minds. What in the hell were we dealing with? Then, when we got to Pine Lawn and found this plethora of nothing but brown ware on the sites, the question was accentuated that this was not Basket Maker stuff. These had to be pit house villages. And we just could not find a handle, a place in the taxonomy of the day to put that material. Then we went south, saw Mogollon 1:15. Once again dominated by plain ware, but there was a little painted ware there; it was red-on-brown. And that was new to us, of course. Then as we visited other sites in the area, we saw a repetition of the same thing at some of the sites, [and the majority of the material was plain ware] but we saw some of the red-on-browns and going into what we consider to be early Mimbres. We knew that Classic Mimbres was at other sites. We figured we had to be dealing with a complex here that was not accommodated in the Pecos classification. We didn't know what to do with it. We decided the only thing to do was to argue it with a shovel. So that's what led to the excavation of the Mogollon 1:15 and Harris sites. (Haury, personal communication 1990)

Although they must have been certain of their discovery, Haury and Gila Pueblo could not just announce to the archaeological community that they had "unearthed" a new culture. It would be another five years before the report documenting that discovery would be published. During the interim, there would be other matters to attend, not the least of which was a doctoral program at Harvard University of Cambridge, Massachusetts.

Interim

Haury had accepted the job at Gila Pueblo with the understanding that Gladwin would permit time off to pursue a PhD, a story Haury (1995) has already recounted. Haury devoted two academic years (1931–33) at Harvard to this purpose, finishing in 1934. In the fall of 1931, the Haurys were at Cambridge for the first year's work. Alfred Marston Tozzer, himself a Harvard alumnus, had been a faculty member there since 1905 and was then the chairman of the department. Although a Mayanist, Tozzer had participated in some important Southwest expeditions, including one to the Rito de los Frijoles, now in Bandelier National Monument, New Mexico. Hulda Haury's diary indicated that her husband had been assigned the Los Muertos material—Los Muertos was a Classic period settlement south of Phoenix, Arizona—as his dissertation topic soon after arriving at Cambridge. Originally, Haury had wanted to pursue tree-ring dating with Egyptian sites, but Tozzer convinced him that the logistical problems would be insurmountable (Haury 1995:718–19). It was Tozzer who proposed Haury study the Hemenway collections that had resided in the Peabody since Frank Hamilton Cushing had excavated them in 1887–88 (Haury 1995:719). Haury must have spent a fair amount of time thinking about the Classic period in Hohokam cultural development as he was completing course assignments and acclimatizing himself to New England and Cambridge.

We have often wondered how the young Haurys—Mennonite midwesterners from the fertile farmlands of Newton, Kansas, who had until recently been residents of the ranching-mining town of Globe, Arizona—adapted to the landscape of the East Coast and the ambience of Harvard University. Although we have been told Emil and Hulda enjoyed the local social life, Haury himself penned a certain apprehension about the Cambridge adventure: "[C]ould an outlander, someone from the Southwest, survive the culture shock in transferring from the informality of Arizona to the staid and conservative cultural environment of New England, and meet the expectations and rigors of a demanding academic routine?" (Haury 1995:714).

We imagine the Harvard landscape was surely a restricted one, centered on the dark basement of the Peabody Museum, the Harvard classrooms and offices, and the Haury apartment in the Holden Green student-housing complex. Even Hulda was confined to the basement, where she helped Emil wash, sort, and mend the ceramic vessels (Haury 1995:721). The brief time spent there surely meant East Coast landscapes influenced Haury less than the wide skies and forested mountains of Arizona and New Mexico. Haury (1995:717) confessed the two years spent at Harvard were traumatic ones, tempered by the kindness and hospitality of Bert and Hattie Cosgrove, dinners with Dr. and Mrs. Tozzer, and teas with Dr. Hooten at his home. The ultimate outcome of being at Harvard was an ulcer that failed to be cured by months of a special diet: "a total and quick cure was effected upon our return to Arizona in late July 1933" (Haury 1995:724), seeming to belie Haury's statement that Harvard was a heady and unforgettable experience.

Although the specific influences of one's professors and fellow students are difficult to gauge, the Harvard intellectual environment did leave significant marks upon the content and direction of Haury's career, if the landscape did not. This influence was clearly the case in the development of his dissertation research, which was directed by Roland B. Dixon and involved the compilation and analysis of information from Los Muertos. Dixon was curator of ethnology at the Peabody Museum. We find it intriguing that Dixon's most important book was *The Building of Cultures*, in which he surveyed the problems of diffusion, independent invention, and environmental influence (Eggan 1968)—topics that Haury himself would later pursue.

During the summer of 1932, Haury returned to Gila Pueblo and fieldwork. He took a small crew, guided by the cowboy Slim Ellison, to the western edge of the Grasshopper Plateau on the Fort Apache Reservation. There, they excavated and sampled roof beams at Canyon Creek Pueblo, a cliff dwelling in the canyon of the same name; we have recounted this story elsewhere (Reid and Whittlesey 1999). The purpose of this project was to give additional research support to Douglass's new method of dating prehistoric ruins. In retrospect, such corroboration would seem unnecessary, except at this time in the early 1930s, only three years after the breakthrough at Show Low, there was considerable skepticism over the validity of Douglass's method. Gladwin, for instance, would perpetuate this disbelief until the late 1940s and would even propose alternative methods of analysis.

Following this interlude, it was back to Harvard for the academic year of 1932–33 to complete course work and finish dissertation research. In the summer of 1933, Haury returned to the Southwest to excavate at Mogollon 1:15, one of the promising pit-house sites he had discovered during the 1931 survey. It was the first of two excavations that would define the Mogollon culture. In May 1934, Haury was back in Cambridge to defend his dissertation. In that work, he presented his and Gladwin's model of the Classic period in Hohokam culture history, which unfortunately was not published until 1945. Not long after, Haury was in New Mexico once more, excavating at the Harris Village, the second project that allowed him to establish and define the Mogollon culture.

Haury would continue this remarkable research agility in switching between Hohokam and Mogollon by supervising the fieldwork of the first major excavation at Snaketown, an enormous Hohokam site along the Gila River in southern Arizona. The work was carried out during the

Figure 4.4 The Gila Pueblo Archaeological Foundation staff at Snaketown in 1935. They are, from left to right, Fisher Motz, Julian Hayden, Evelyn Dennis, E. B. Sayles, Erik Reed, Nancy Pinkley, Irwin Hayden, and Emil Haury. (Courtesy of the Arizona State Museum; neg. no. 70551)

winter of 1934–35 after completing the Harris Village excavations (fig. 4.4). The monumental Snaketown report would allow Gladwin and Haury to complete a full description and culture history for the Hohokam as well as set in motion an entirely different set of contentious issues. For the next two years at Gila Pueblo and for much of the rest of his archaeological career, Haury would juggle the Mogollon and Hohokam culture concepts. But first came the Mogollon, and we turn next to the sites that gave birth to the Mogollon concept and Haury's stunning, iconoclastic, and controversial report—*The Mogollon Culture of Southwestern New Mexico.*

5
Defining the Mogollon Culture

> Gila Pueblo was much more than just the impact of its
> geographic setting, but one cannot dissociate its physical
> location from its stellar professional reputation, the
> dedication of its staff, and its freedom to act without being
> unduly influenced by federal, state, and political constraints.
>
> —Emil Haury (1988:ix)

New Mexico—even the name is evocative, hinting of exotic lands improbably hidden deep in the American West. It is possibly the most quintessential southwestern place, capturing the essence of Pueblo cultures and Spanish Colonial history in a landscape of fierce light and red earth. Its houses and pueblo towns lie close to the land, clinging to sheer rock mesas or mounding subtly on the earth from which they are made. Blue-black mountain ranges cut into skies of evanescent blue. Over it all lingers the scents of cinnamon and roasted chile wafting from the *cocinas*, burning piñon, and the cold fragrance of snow-covered stone.

The southwestern corner of this magical land is mountain country. Ranges and ridges roll endlessly into the distance. Snowmelt in the Gila and Mogollon mountains feeds the San Francisco, Mimbres, and Gila rivers, and from the rivers spill Cameron, Sapillo, and Mule creeks. In a few choice places, the river valleys widen to offer farmland. This rugged country provided substance and shelter for one of the Southwest's most mobile and least agricultural ancient people, the mountain Mogollon. During the survey of discovery in 1931, Haury took a special interest in two of the many Mogollon sites that he and his companion, Hastings, had recorded—Mogollon Village, overlooking the San Francisco River some ten miles north of Glenwood, New Mexico, and Harris Village, located on the Mimbres River about seventy-five miles southeast of Mogollon Village.

These two pit-house villages may appear innocuous, but the report that Haury penned after excavating them in the summers of 1933 and 1934 incited a storm of controversy that was not quieted for decades. In this chapter, we seek to convey what Haury discovered and why he thought these two sites were sufficiently distinctive to require the definition of a new cultural phenomenon that would set the American archaeological world astir—the Mogollon culture.

Mogollon and Harris Villages

Mogollon Village lies atop a mesa above the San Francisco River. The river can be seen meandering a bit to the north before its course disappears. Below, leafy cottonwoods refresh eyes weary from the incessant light. In June, they seem to spring from the riverbank like billowy, green thunderheads. The Mogollon Mountains rise to the east; to the west and northwest, broken ridges and hills separate the San Francisco and Blue river drainages. The rugged, dissected landscape belies the fact that this is desert country—dry, and in the summer, hot, as we discovered one day in June 2000. We fought our way through scrubby juniper, mesquite, and cactus to reach the flat mesa top, sweating and out of breath. As Haury noted in his report on the site, it is inaccessible from all sides but one. The locale commands an outstanding view of the river below and the foothills of the mountain ranges. It would be difficult to imagine a more suitable place to live, if one were a casual farmer heavily invested in hunting the region's abundant game, collecting its rich plant resources, and seeking safety for family and stored foods.

The Harris Village, labeled New Mexico Q:1:14 in the Gila Pueblo site-numbering system, was the second site Haury excavated, and it is located in a different setting. The surrounding country is just as rugged as that near Mogollon Village, but the site is situated on an open, level terrace, and the river valley is broad and open. Scrubby, piñon-juniper woodland covers the site area, and a dense riparian zone with cottonwood, walnut, and other trees lines the riverbanks. Today, neither site hints at the archaeological riches hidden below. In general, pit structures give few indications of their presence from the surface—perhaps a depression, possibly a subtle difference in soil or vegetation—and time has erased most traces of the excavations.

On August 1, 1933, Haury and Hastings established a camp among the piñon trees near the highway and about ten minutes' walk to the site, and work began on the Mogollon Village. Two O'odham laborers from Blackwater, Arizona, and James Simmons, an avocational archaeologist from Prescott who would make outstanding contributions to archaeology in his own right, made up the initial crew. Haury (1979) remembered that Gladwin, Mrs. MacCurdy, and Donald Scott, director of Harvard's Peabody Museum, visited during fieldwork and shared the excitement of the intriguing finds. "Each day's work produced new surprises," Haury (1979:93) recalled. Work continued until mid-September 1933.

Sometime in the winter of 1933–34, Haury may have had an inkling of the controversy to come. He recalled to Reid (Haury 1979) that after the work at Mogollon Village, the suspicions aroused on the 1931 survey that the Mogollon were distinctive were reaffirmed, and the material provided a better body of data to work with. After that, Haury said, "I invited Earl Morris, who of course was a dyed in the wool Anasazi–Basket Maker type. And I said, 'Earl, we've got some stuff down here that you can't simply put in the Basket Maker category. I wish you would come down and excavate that site in the Forestdale Valley'" (Haury, personal communication 1990). This took place in 1934, before the Harris site was excavated. Earl H. Morris was born in New Mexico and was considered by his peers the consummate "dirt archaeologist" (Fowler 2000:290). Educated at the University of Colorado, Morris is known for his work at the massive Chaco Canyon outlier site of Aztec, New Mexico, but it was his knowledge of Basketmaker culture in the La Plata district of southern Colorado for which Haury sought his opinion.

Although Morris expressed some interest, it of course was Haury himself who would investigate the Mogollon sites of the Forestdale Valley. Haury's attempt to enlist the aid of a recognized Anasazi scholar at this early time may reflect a prescient knowledge of his rueful observation decades later that "Archaeologists soon learn that the usual professional reaction to innovations is negative" (Haury 1979:97).

Harris Village, located on the property of Mrs. John Q. Harris about one-quarter mile east of the Mimbres Post Office, was excavated in the summer of 1934. Mrs. Harris agreed to allow the excavations in return for the sum of one dollar and the promise that she would be allowed to keep any gold, silver, or other precious metals the archaeologists discovered. For several years, the Laboratory of Anthropology in Santa Fe had offered scholarships for Training in Anthropological Field Methods. In 1934, Haury was invited to take its scholars as crew members, allowing him to excavate the Harris Village. Haury recalled that "The energy expended by those fellows matched or exceeded that of any team I ever had." Many of their names will be familiar to archaeologists—Gordon C. Baldwin of the University of Arizona, Gordon F. Ekholm representing the University of Minnesota, Norman E. Gabel of Harvard University, Deric Nusbaum, and Erik K. Reed. Reed, Haury's fellow student at Harvard, would go on to be one of the Mogollon's greatest supporters, arguing vehemently against those who would subsume it as a backwater variant of Anasazi.

In describing those initial excavations to Reid, Haury said:

> We had something that we had to recognize was different from Basket Maker, and in toying around with an idea what to call it, it was in the Mogollon Mountains where this stuff seemed to be, so let's give it that name. And, of course, as you can imagine, there was considerable resistance to it. But I could always come back with the fact that this isn't Basket Maker. You can't by any stretch of the imagination make this stuff out as Basket Maker as defined by the Pecos classification. So what is it? And it is not the red-on-buff stuff from the desert, so it is something else. So we figured we were justified in giving it another name. (Haury, personal communication 1990)

In 1936, Haury did precisely that. The report of the excavations at Mogollon and Harris Villages, *The Mogollon Culture of Southwestern New Mexico*, claimed discovery of a new culture for the prehistoric Southwest. This was also the year that Kidder introduced "Anasazi" as a substitute label for Basketmaker-Pueblo. Based on excavations at the Mogollon and Harris pit-house villages and extensive surveys of the central mountains and southern deserts, Haury made assertions that would upset his colleagues and fuel two decades of controversy. We catalog here some of the more crucial aspects of the Mogollon culture that made it seem so radically different from Basketmaker-Pueblo and Hohokam that Haury felt it had to be labeled something else, chiefly architecture, pottery, and mortuary practices.

Dating Mogollon and Harris Villages

Ceramics and stratigraphy were the chief means by which Mogollon and Harris villages were dated, as only a few tree-ring dates were obtained. Haury used sherds found within 10 cm of the floor and whole vessels, when they were present, to date the structures. No tree-ring dates were obtained from Harris Village, and only four from houses at Mogollon Village. They fell within the San Francisco phase between AD 896 and 908. Haury noted that intrusive ceramic types provided only suggestive clues for site dating. In the end, he concluded that the San Francisco phase was generally coeval with Pueblo I (AD 700–900) in the Pecos classification, and the Three Circle phase was broadly contemporaneous with the Pueblo II period (AD 900–1150). He thought that the earliest phase, Georgetown, "may well extend into Basketmaker III" (Haury, in Reid and Doyel 1986:395). Mogollon Village was more short-lived than Harris Village; it was occupied from the Georgetown through the San Francisco phases. Occupation at Harris Village extended into the Three Circle phase.

Haury attempted to establish the antiquity of the Mogollon culture by comparing it to the as-yet-unpublished information from Snaketown. There, he noted, the only "foreign" ceramics found in early levels were those of the Mogollon culture, and in several cases, these sherds appeared in strata predating northern intrusive sherds. Thus, at or before AD 700, three broad types of pottery were being made, the black-on-white of the late Basketmakers, the earliest red-painted Hohokam types, and the red-on-brown of the Mogollon. To Haury, this indicated that "three major groups shared in the structure of the rather complex southwestern picture." Subsequently, critics would return repeatedly to the dating of the Mogollon culture in an attempt to discredit its antiquity.

Architecture

Once, twenty pit structures were scattered about the mesa top on which Mogollon Village was situated; of these, Haury excavated eleven. Harris Village was larger than Mogollon Village; Haury estimated it contained more than a hundred structures, of which thirty-four were excavated. The typical Mogollon dwelling was a pit structure—a foundation was dug into the earth and covered with a superstructure of poles, grass, and mud. The floor was thus below ground. Sloping, rather than stepped, and covered passageways provided entrance into the house. Mogollon structures were so-called true pit houses, in which the support posts for the side walls were placed outside the pit on the ground surface. The pit excavated as a foundation was deep, and the entries were relatively narrow and long.

House shapes at both sites were highly variable, and shape changed through time. Round and bean-shaped houses—the latter so named because the entry and its adobe-plastered corner posts shaped an indentation into one long, or lateral, side—were early, shifting to subrectangular and rectangular shapes through time. At Harris Village, some houses were lined with cobble masonry, which Haury suggested was designed to stabilize the soft, earthen side walls. Hearths inside the houses were shallow depressions located in line with the entrance.

Haury suggested that some houses probably were ceremonial structures. Although constructed much like habitations, these structures were much larger, and the support posts were "massive." There were round and rectangular forms, and none of the architectural features characteristic of puebloan kivas were present. Therefore, Haury noted that although these structures probably were analogous to kivas in function, they could not be labeled as such.

The characteristics of true-pit-house architecture—deep pit, long and sloping entry, and round or bean shape—differed strongly from Hohokam architecture as Haury had encountered it firsthand at Roosevelt 9:6 in the Tonto Basin. Hohokam pit structures were more properly called "houses in pits," because the walls were set inside the foundation pit, which usually was shallow. The typical house was subrectangular with rounded corners. Haury (in Reid and Doyel 1986:369) stated these distinctions succinctly. "The form, the gable type of roof, the position of the firepit, and the entrance through the side, are parallel. The entrance passage in the Hohokam area, however, shows a great reduction in length and is equipped with a step rather than a graded floor, this feature being obviated by the shallowness of the house pit." Haury also noted that the developmental sequence of house shape was opposite to that seen in Hohokam architecture.

There also were differences between the architecture of the Mogollon and Harris villages and Anasazi pit structures. Comparing the contemporaneous Pueblo I structures at the Kiatuthlanna site in eastern Arizona, Haury noted that several features were not duplicated at the Mogollon sites. These included roof entrances, benches, and a four-post roof-support system. Expanding the comparison to include other sites, Haury (in Reid and Doyel 1986:371) observed that interior furnishings such as deflectors, ventilators, antechambers, *sipapus* (small, central depressions), and other features were not found in the Mogollon and Harris villages.

Ceramics

It was the plain brown pottery of the mountain settlements that initially drew the attention of Haury and Hastings during their 1931 survey of discovery. Ceramics recovered during the 1933 and 1934 excavations proved the distinctiveness of Mogollon wares. In the earliest phases, only brown plain ware (Alma Plain and several variants) and polished and slipped red ware with a brown paste (San Francisco Red) were present. Later, a well-polished ware with linear, geometric designs in red paint (Mogollon Red-on-brown) was made. The plain ware was dark and fire clouded, the product of a poorly controlled, oxidizing firing atmosphere, and frequently was scored heavily. Sometimes punctated and incised decorations were used. Plain ware jars with banded or corrugated necks also were manufactured. All types were made by coiling and finished by pinching and scraping.

Haury was able to demonstrate with stratigraphy and stylistic patterns a developmental sequence in painted ware. Mogollon Red-on-brown pottery was followed by a short-lived, red-on-white ware (Three Circle Red-on-white), which itself gave rise to the characteristic Mimbres Black-on-white pottery that was well known before Haury began his excavations.

The materials and technology of Mogollon ceramics contrasted strongly with that of Hohokam and Anasazi pottery. All prehistoric ceramics of the Southwest were made by coiling, but the method by which the coils were bonded together and smoothed differed among cultures. Hohokam pottery was bonded and smoothed by the paddle-and-anvil technique. Although the plain ware had a brown paste, the painted ware was made from distinctive, buff-firing clay, and red ware was extremely rare. Anasazi pottery was made by coiling, and the coils were bonded and smoothed by pinching and scraping. The clay was sedimentary and iron poor, which in combination with a reducing firing atmosphere, yielded a gray ware. Mogollon pottery was made by coiling and scraping, and it was fabricated from brown-firing clay of igneous origin. Polishing and texturing were characteristic of Mogollon wares, but were little used in Hohokam and Anasazi pottery. The Mogollon painted and red wares were polished heavily, so much so that they sometimes exhibited a "hammered," or dimpled, effect, the result of polishing over the indentations left from pinching the coils together.

To Haury, the construction methods were particularly important in distinguishing Mogollon ceramics from the pottery made by the Hohokam and the Anasazi. Haury noted (in Reid and Doyel 1986:398–99) strong similarities between Mogollon ceramics, those of the Dragoon and San Simon cultures of southeastern Arizona, and northern Chihuahua ceramics. Haury wrote (in Reid and Doyel 1986:399), "practically the entire ceramic complex of painted, red, plain, and textured wares reverts directly back to the Mogollon substructure (Sayles 1936)." These observations would be confirmed decades later (Heckman, Montgomery, and Whittlesey 2000; Whittlesey 2004b).

In the companion volume on the pottery from the Mogollon and Harris villages, Haury expanded upon these points and presented a few more. He noted that Mogollon pottery was of respectable antiquity, being technically proficient as early as the Georgetown phase. Mogollon pottery was the foundation from which numerous red ware, brown plain ware, and red-on-brown ceramics in southeastern Arizona and southwestern New Mexico developed. He also noted that certain styles of decoration on Anasazi painted ceramics were derived from the Mogollon, whereas many characteristics of Mimbres Bold Face Black-on-white resembled Hohokam painted decoration. The developmental sequence from red-on-brown through black-on-white pottery casts doubt on the Anasazi swamping theory later developed to characterize the post–AD 1000 Mogollon.

Mortuary Practices

The Mogollon buried their deceased. Eight inhumations were discovered at Mogollon Village, and forty-eight were found at the much larger Harris Village. Burials were scattered about the village at both sites and were placed in abandoned houses or storage pits. The bodies were arranged in flexed, semiflexed, or extended positions; the flexed inhumations were placed in a sitting posture or on the back. Orientation was often to the east, but there was much variation, leading Haury (in Reid and Doyel 1986:373) to state that "orientation was not dictated by custom." Grave goods were few and sometimes ritually "killed" by deliberately punching a hole in the bottom of a metate or ceramic bowl.

These practices contrasted directly with Hohokam customs. The Hohokam cremated their dead, placing the remains in pits or occasionally in ceramic urns. Spatially distinct cemeteries were reserved for burials; only rarely were cremations placed inside abandoned structures. Long after Haury worked at Snaketown, researchers would suggest that cremation cemeteries were associated with kinship or residential groups. Ceramics usually accompanied Hohokam burials, but they were often deliberately broken; ornaments also were common accompaniments. At Snaketown, lavish concentrations of projectile points and shell ornaments would be found in some burials. The Mogollon used cremation only rarely; one secondary pit cremation was found at Mogollon Village and two at Harris Village, and we cannot be sure that co-residing people of different affiliation were not responsible for these cremations. Haury noted (in Reid and Doyel 1986:398) that the Basketmaker-Pueblo peoples also practiced inhumation, and there was more similarity in mortuary practices between Mogollon and Basketmaker-Pueblo than Mogollon and Hohokam.

Haury (in Reid and Doyel 1986:373) observed that a change to sub-floor, intramural inhumation began in the Three Circle phase and became the common practice by the Mimbres phase. Offerings also increased in frequency and variety. Ceremonial killing of grave goods first took place in the San Francisco phase, when entire vessels were deliberately broken, and the pieces scattered in the grave. Later work by Anyon (1980) and Anyon and LeBlanc (1986) confirmed Haury's observations on these changes.

Other Material Culture

In certain aspects, Mogollon and Anasazi flaked and ground stone tools corresponded (Haury, in Reid and Doyel 1986:386–87). They shared full-grooved mauls, short pipes, and one-ended trough metates. By contrast, "the Mogollon people possessed the hoe, stone bowls, long stone pipes," and "a slightly differing projectile point." At that time, it was thought that Anasazi and Mogollon lacked three-quarter-grooved axes and slate palettes, which Haury believed were "two characteristics of the Hohokam, whose stonework at an early date excelled in kind and form that ever produced by either the Basketmaker-Pueblo [Anasazi] or the Mogollon people" (Haury, in Reid and Doyel 1986:387). Subsequent research would discover hoes and three-quarter-grooved axes to be present. Hoes would be found primarily in the Mimbres Classic period in caches, and full-grooved and three-quarter-grooved axes would be found in the Mimbres region during the Late Pit House and Mimbres Classic periods (Anyon and LeBlanc 1986). Much later, in his return to Snaketown, Haury (1976) would demonstrate that slate palettes and censers were used together in

Hohokam rituals. The few palettes found in the Mimbres region may have been imports from the Hohokam region (Anyon and LeBlanc 1986).

As to shell ornaments, Haury again noted differences with the Hohokam: in the Gila River Basin, "the stage of great richness and multiplicity of objects produced was somewhat ahead of that in the Mimbres" (Haury in Reid and Doyel 1986:388). This typical Haury understatement belies the enormous emphasis the Hohokam placed on marine-shell ornaments, which were so vital as to suggest they were emblematic of Hohokam identity and represented fundamental ideological and cosmological notions (Whittlesey 2003).

The Mogollon Culture

Introducing the conclusions to the report of excavations at Mogollon and Harris villages, Haury wrote:

> At the close of the first field season in the Mogollon Village, an initial difficulty was experienced in attempting to relate the remains to either of the two currently recognized culture groups in the Southwest, the Hohokam, on the one hand, and the Basketmaker-Pueblo on the other. The difficulty was not lessened after excavating in the Harris Village. The problem of relationship resolved itself into three questions: Were the remains to be regarded as a peripheral variation of the Basketmaker-Pueblo complex of the north; of the Hohokam to the west; or was a third basic group represented which, up to this stage in the investigations, had not been recognized? (Haury, in Reid and Doyel 1986:396)

The way in which Haury went about answering these questions was characteristic of the scholarly personality he would display throughout his career. He marshaled the evidence, which had been produced by intensive excavation. First, Haury summarized elements of the Georgetown and San Francisco phases, which he believed characterized "the culture type possessed by the occupants of the Mogollon and Harris villages" (in Reid and Doyel 1986:397). He considered subsistence, physical type, interment practices, architecture, storage pits, pottery, ground stone, and flaked stone artifacts and added what was known of shell and bone objects.

Second, Haury proceeded with care to compare and contrast these elements with what was known to date of the Hohokam. (Recall that excavations at Snaketown did not begin until the winter of 1934–35, after the work at Harris Village was finished; the Snaketown report was published in 1937. In writing the Mogollon report, Haury occasionally drew upon observations derived from the Snaketown excavations.) His comparisons demonstrated little, if any, similarities between Mogollon and Hohokam. Turning to the Basketmaker-Pueblo, Haury wrote that "a somewhat closer relationship is apparent," but there were nevertheless "elementary differences" in "architecture, in the stone culture, and especially in pottery" (in Reid and Doyel 1986:398). Haury concluded (in Reid and Doyel 1986:398): "The manifestations of the culture, both racial and material, are neither Basketmaker nor Hohokam as now defined, and it cannot be equated with either without many qualifications. It is therefore felt that a logical solution lies in the recognition of a third group—The Mogollon Culture."

Haury then proceeded to make two statements that would generate controversy. Not only was Mogollon distinctive, it also was as old as Basketmaker, and it exerted strong influences on neighboring regions. Citing previous Medallion Papers published by Gila Pueblo, Haury (in Reid and Doyel 1986:398) wrote that "Practically all villages of the eleventh to fifteenth centuries which lay to the west, south, and east of the Mimbres area proper were founded on the Mogollon complex." In addition, the phase chart revising the original given in Medallion Paper 15 placed Mogollon side by side with the Chaco Branch and began both in Basketmaker III times (Haury, in Reid and Doyel 1986:399).

A final claim for Mogollon distinctiveness was based on what Haury saw as its "eastern" connections, by which he meant "a Plains group in a hunting-agricultural stage" (in Reid and Doyel 1986:401). In Gladwin's view, Mogollon was derived out of what was labeled the Caddoan Root. In the first mention of Mogollon in print, Gladwin (Gladwin and Gladwin 1934:30–31) classified Mogollon as a branch of the Playas Stem of the Caddoan Root, and commented that "Reports on the entire series of the Mogollon and Chihuahua Branches of the Playas Stem are now in preparation." The Caddoan connection quickly dropped from the list of Mogollon traits; it was one of Gladwin's more fanciful notions, rather than a fact of the archaeological record.

Haury closed this remarkable report with a summary of Mimbres prehistory, which emphasized its Mogollon character in the early stages and proposed a suite of cultural influences beginning about AD 900 that "completely altered the complexion of the group" (Haury, in Reid and

Doyel 1986:402). Aboveground, masonry pueblos replaced pit structures, and black-on-white pottery was made, instead of the red-on-brown pottery of Mogollon authorship. Both were attributed to "Pueblo" or Anasazi influence. To the end of his life, Haury remained firm in his conviction that once masonry pueblos and black-on-white pottery appeared, the Mogollon culture was submerged in a wave of Puebloan influences and could no longer properly be labeled Mogollon. In 1985, for example, he wrote: "I cringe . . . when the large, late pueblos like Tundastusa, Grasshopper, Kinishba, and Point of Pines Ruin are labeled as Mogollon, or when St. Johns Polychrome is called a Mogollon pottery type" (Haury 1985a:404).

In slightly more than 100 pages published in 1936, Haury had laid out a coherent argument for defining a new prehistoric culture of the Southwest that would turn the archaeological world upside down. The major points that would prove to be so controversial to his colleagues were: (1) Mogollon should be recognized as a third culture equivalent to Basketmaker-Pueblo and Hohokam; (2) Mogollon was at least as old as the Basketmakers; and (3) its basic character was, late in time, submerged by a number of Basketmaker-Pueblo traits. The controversy soon to develop revolved around the first two claims, those concerning separateness and antiquity, or, more generally, taxonomy and chronology. The degree of submergence in or amalgamation with the Anasazi became an issue dividing those who believed in the Mogollon culture.

From our perspective in the twenty-first century, in a postmodern era that includes metaphor, symbol, agency, and practice in archaeological discourse, the concern with cultural definition and taxonomy seems quaint. We would do well to recall that in essence, southwestern archaeology *was* taxonomy at that time in its history. The Pecos classification stemming from the first Pecos Conference of 1927 was the ultimate arbiter of cultural status, and it had been developed when southwestern archaeologists had barely stepped off the Colorado Plateau. Researchers were only beginning to explore other regions, but the findings of the Laboratory of Anthropology in Santa Fe and the Museum of Northern Arizona, among others, were starting to confirm what the Gila Pueblo archaeologists knew to be true: the archaeological record of the desert and mountain regions did not fit the Pecos mold. Haury (1985a:xv) recalled the dilemma: "[I]f the Pecos agreement was to apply to the Southwest as a whole, either its guidelines would need modification to accommodate the later findings or new categories in the system of classification were necessary. The steady accumulation of information soon demonstrated that the latter alternative was the route to pursue."

We would also do well to remember that at the time, southwestern archaeology was conducted by consensus and by the strength of the archaeologist's personality and intellect. Placed in this context, *The Mogollon Culture of Southwestern New Mexico* can be seen as an attempt to provide the necessary new modifications to accommodate Haury's discoveries at the Mogollon and Harris villages. It also was a well-considered effort to convince his colleagues of the propriety and necessity of his new world order. As we shall see, only some of Haury's colleagues were convinced.

The report also is extraordinary for having been written twice. In the summer of 1935, the Gladwins were camped at Red Mesa east of Gallup. Gladwin called Haury in Globe, asking for the Mogollon report to look over. In those days, of course, copy machines were yet to be invented, and manuscripts were laboriously typed with carbon paper if one wanted a copy. Haury recalled that he sent the report with "great trepidation," shorn of its illustrations. In August, Gladwin called again with the horrifying news that their camp had burned along with the Mogollon manuscript. There was nothing to do but settle down to recreating the original. Haury admitted that the final results were the better for the rewriting. It is no coincidence that, looking back over the history of southwestern archaeology, we see no single idea that created a greater furor than that of the Mogollon culture, and not until the "New Archaeology" of the 1960s did one so polarize southwestern archaeologists.

6
The Gathering Storm of Controversy

> It always seemed paradoxical to me that there should have
> been so much resistance to recognizing multiple cultural
> groups in antiquity, when historically we can tally a dozen or
> more Indian tribes in the Southwest with almost as many life
> styles and half as many distinct language groupings.
>
> —Emil Haury (1985a:xvi)

By the time *The Mogollon Culture of Southwestern New Mexico* appeared in 1936, Haury already had moved into new directions. In the winter of 1934–35, he had directed excavations at the monumental Hohokam site of Snaketown along the middle Gila River in the Phoenix area. Preparing the report of this work would occupy the next two years of his life. In 1936, Haury and E. B. "Ted" Sayles excavated at White Mound, a late Basketmaker III village on the Puerco River near Gallup. It was to be Haury's final project for Gila Pueblo. In 1937, when the Snaketown monograph was published and just one year after reporting his identification and definition of the Mogollon culture, Haury left Gila Pueblo to become head of the Department of Archaeology at the University of Arizona, replacing his mentor, Cummings. In the following year, he would take over as director of the Arizona State Museum.

These events no doubt overshadowed the effects Haury's monograph created in the archaeological community. It is clear, however, that Haury may have not anticipated the mixed reviews of and negative reception to the proposed Mogollon culture, and that his response to the critique was visceral and heartfelt, to the extent that he devoted much of his professional life to vindicating the concept.

The Scholars Weigh In

The initial reviews of *The Mogollon Culture of Southwestern New Mexico* were positive. In the year following the publication, Paul Sidney Martin (1937:233) reviewed it as "so astonishing, so far-reaching, and so unorthodox that the worth of this report and of the new data contained herein probably will not be understood or esteemed for some years." Prophetically, Martin anticipated that "the hypothesis set forth in this excellent report will doubtless be scoffed at by many competent people." Events would soon prove Martin correct, and his own research would place him beside Haury firmly in the midst of the ensuing controversy. Frank H. H. Roberts's (1937) summary of southwestern archaeology was less enthusiastic than Martin's review, although he did give the Mogollon treatment equivalent to that of the Anasazi and Hohokam. It took little time, however, for a critical tone to enter the literature.

In 1938, Paul Nesbitt reported his work on the Starkweather Ruin. This multiple-component site located near Reserve, New Mexico, had pit structures dating to the Georgetown, San Francisco, and Three Circle phases, as well as a Reserve phase pueblo. To Nesbitt (1938), the Mogollon did not represent a new culture; its elements were similar and in many cases identical to Anasazi, with some ideas borrowed from the Hohokam. He also saw Mogollon as no older that Pueblo I (AD 700–900) in the Pecos classification. Importantly, Nesbitt discredited the antiquity of Mogollon pottery. Because Nesbitt did not believe in the legitimacy of Mogollon, the presence of San Francisco Red at Snaketown could only mean that Hohokam and Mogollon received pottery technology from an outside, undisclosed source. Nesbitt appears to have been influenced by Kidder, who viewed the material remains that Haury labeled Mogollon as the result of mixing of Anasazi and Hohokam traits.

The following year, Kidder, who was widely considered the patriarch of southwestern archaeology, reviewed Nesbitt's report. Kidder (1939:315–16) wrote that the Mogollon mountain folk were "receptive rather than radiating"; he believed they lacked individuality and had all the earmarks of a peripheral, borrowing culture. Only the early pottery was distinctive, but Kidder echoed Nesbitt's belief that the ceramics derived from an outside source, presumably in Mexico. "If this be true," Kidder (1939:316) concluded, then "Mogollon loses its sole significant claim to individuality." Nesbitt had dismissed the pottery issue with the assertion that "culture cannot be solely defined in terms of pottery and the true perspective and picture of the situation is likely to become lost in making ceramics alone the archaeological objective" (Nesbitt 1938:83). Much later, Haury would write concerning this issue:

> I am well aware that pottery cannot always be used as a certain identifier of a people, but one need look only at the pottery produced today by southwestern Indians to realize that there is a one-to-one correlation between type and tribe for most of the vessels produced. I believe that this situation obtained in antiquity as well, and that the inference that Anasazi-Mogollon ceramic differences denote "tribal" differences is sound. (1985a:xvii)

In this opinion, Haury foreshadowed the views of later twentieth-century anthropologists who would develop the concept of "technological style"— a distinctive way of doing a task, whether building a pueblo or flaking a stone tool, which differentiated among learning frameworks and therefore social traditions.

In Nesbitt's and Kidder's arguments, we can clearly see the influence of the Anasazi bias; until Gila Pueblo and other institutions began to probe the desert and mountain regions of the Southwest, the Anasazi of the Colorado Plateau were considered to be its sole legitimate archaeological culture. From this point of view, it was only natural that cultural manifestations differing from Anasazi would be considered nothing more than variants of that culture or largely influenced by it. Both Nesbitt and Kidder appear to have underplayed the significant point of Haury's intimate involvement with Hohokam and to a somewhat lesser extent, Anasazi archaeology as well as Mogollon. Haury's adventures in northeastern Arizona following Cummings's directives, and his work at Tusayan Ruin and White Mound had familiarized him with the Anasazi; from his excavations at Roosevelt 9:6 and Snaketown, he knew the Hohokam. Most important, Haury had surveyed most of the Southwest and more distant regions in search of the elusive Red-on-Buff culture. With such experience under his belt—experience that his colleagues lacked—Haury alone was capable of making the provocative assessments of the 1936 report.

Two questions marked the initial phases of the Mogollon controversy. First, were the mountain people sufficiently distinct from the Anasazi as to require a new label? Second, if they were that distinct, were the Mogollon to be viewed as a culture equivalent to the Anasazi and Hohokam? The antiquity of Mogollon pottery was also under fire. Pottery was the hallmark of southwestern culture, despite Nesbitt's statements to the contrary, and it was the principal ingredient of archaeological reconstruction then as now. Anasazi archaeologists did not warm to the prospect of the mountain people Kidder had characterized as more or less "backward" making pottery before the Anasazi.

Answers to both questions were muddled by the intimate relationship of Mogollon to Hohokam. Although culturally distinct from Hohokam, Mogollon was closely tied to this newly revealed, ceramic-producing neighbor of the Arizona desert. Mogollon pottery alone was found associated with the earliest Hohokam wares. Additionally, both Mogollon and Hohokam were identified and defined through the fieldwork of Gila Pueblo. It was a private, nonacademic institution whose director, Gladwin, lacked academic credentials and any formal training in archaeology. A subtext of the controversy was beginning to take shape, one that involved scholarship beyond the bounds of established intellectual traditions at a time when American archaeology needed to legitimize its academic standing.

In addition to the valid questions of determining distinctiveness and antiquity and a self-conscious concern with academic legitimacy, there began to creep into the controversy elements of opinion and faith apart from an objective, scientific evaluation of the evidence. Belief born of faith as well as sheer stubbornness would fuel both sides of the argument for many years to come. Among the first articles of faith to emerge was a reluctance to modify the hypothesis of the Anasazi as culture bearer to the Southwest. The personality and authority of the remarkable Kidder are linked to this conservative stance. Morris depicted the issue succinctly:

> Most of us under the grip of the northern bias were content to accept the Basketmaker-Pueblo cycle as basic, presumably representative of neighboring districts which had not yet been measured by its standards, and probably parental to the relatively late culture variants known to have existed in regions to the southeast, south and southwest of the San Juan center.
>
> It remained for the Gladwins and their co-workers of Gila Pueblo to jar the kaleidoscope. Disturb the picture they certainly have, not in the sense of disrupting the San Juan sequence, but by showing that there are major provinces in the Southwest to which it is not applicable. Due to their efforts the Hohokam of the Gila are as firmly established as are the Basketmaker-Pueblo of the north. . . . Gila Pueblo

advocates a third parent stem in the Southwestern complex—the Mogollon culture of southwestern New Mexico. . . . The claims of the Mogollon culture to fundamental individuality and antiquity so far are not as well confirmed as those of the Hohokam. It is, however, the opinion of Gladwin and Haury that additional excavation would carry it back to parallel the earliest Hohokam phase now known. No clearer minds than theirs have grappled with Southwestern problems, and in regard to this point, I would expect time to prove them right. (Morris 1939:248)

Most southwestern archaeologists, of course, were "under the grip of the northern bias" because that was where most of the fieldwork had been done. The southern portion of the Colorado Plateau, the San Juan River drainage, was a monumental landscape of spectacular pueblo ruins made interpretable by years of exploration, excellent preservation, an abundance of tree-ring dates, and contemporary Pueblo Indians, who provided direct analogies into the prehistoric past. Anasazi archaeologists were justifiably proud and notoriously self-centered. In 1924, Kidder had written *An Introduction to the Study of Southwestern Archaeology*, the first regional synthesis produced in North America, and in 1927, he had convened the first Pecos Conference to codify a classification system for the Basketmaker-Pueblo cultural sequence. Soon after the 1929 tree-ring breakthrough by Douglass, the periods of the Pecos classification and the major pueblo ruins could be assigned absolute dates in the Christian calendar. In 1936, the same year Haury had written the Mogollon report, Kidder introduced the Navajo word "Anasazi" as a shorthand label for Basketmaker-Pueblo. Anasazi archaeologists were years ahead of any other regional group in North America, and there was no need to disbelieve the promise of continued leadership of the southwestern archaeological community.

Kidder had closed his long-term field project at Pecos Pueblo in 1929 and was in the throes of analyzing and reporting on this important work. In 1939, Brew concluded the Harvard Peabody Museum's five-year Awat'ovi project, which also investigated pueblos and pit-house villages on Antelope Mesa in the Hopi country. During a decade of nationwide economic depression, southwestern archaeology had made major advances in data collection and classification and was poised to interpret the past.

Haury Returns to the University of Arizona

By 1939, only three years after the publication of *The Mogollon Culture of Southwestern New Mexico*, Haury was in a leadership position that permitted him to establish his own research agenda. As head of the recently renamed Anthropology Department at the University of Arizona and director of the Arizona State Museum, he was in a command position to direct archaeological research toward questions of his choosing.

White Mound had signaled the end of Haury's involvement with Gila Pueblo. Although he and Sayles had been dispatched to collect the information, architectural data, artifacts, and tree-ring specimens that Gladwin wanted, and Gladwin had visited the excavations, if only rarely, it was Gladwin who would write the report. We imagine that Haury must have felt this injustice keenly. Haury recalled that he had been oblivious to Cummings's advanced age and the need to find his replacement at the University of Arizona until Cummings visited Haury in Globe in November 1936. There, Cummings proposed that Haury take the position of head of the Department of Archaeology.

Haury spent an uneasy winter awaiting a formal offer, as his relationship with Gladwin became increasingly strained. In the spring, the offer finally arrived, and a relieved Haury began to conclude his affairs at Gila Pueblo. On July 1, 1937, he assumed the headship of the Department of Archaeology at the age of thirty-three. His first act was to rename it the Department of Anthropology.

Shortly after, Haury began to establish long-term research agendas for his newly renamed department. In 1938, Haury initiated an anthropological study program on what was then called the Papago Indian Reservation, now the Tohono O'odham Nation (Reid 2008). A joint project of the Department of Anthropology and the Arizona State Museum, the long-term, multidisciplinary Papaguería Project was designed to research the history of the Native Americans of southern Arizona and their prehistoric predecessors. Physical anthropology, ethnography, and archaeology were components of the program. The latter included Haury's famous excavations at Ventana Cave, the report of which was published in 1950. With the Papaguería Project, Haury expanded his interests in issues of Hohokam origins and continuity with contemporary peoples of the desert.

It also had become apparent to Haury that acceptance of the Mogollon concept required more fieldwork. In his introduction to the Bear Village report, originally published in 1940, Haury (1985a:140) wrote, "The writer was further encouraged to continue studies on the Mogollon problem by the insistence of many of those who attended the 1938 Chaco Canyon Conference of the University of New Mexico. It was felt that only further work could clear it up." Steeped in an empiricist tradition and conditioned by his years at Gila Pueblo to argue points with the shovel, Haury also was ready to try his hand at training young archaeologists in a summer field-school program. The Papaguería project fulfilled this goal during the winter months, but in the summer, the Forestdale Valley beckoned.

As we have seen, Haury had hoped that Morris, who was a highly respected Anasazi expert, would tackle the Mogollon problem with excavations in the Forestdale Valley (Haury 1985a:139). Gladwin had suggested to Morris that Forestdale was an ideal place to test Morris's theories concerning the development of pottery technology. Haury had faith that Morris would arrive at conclusions similar to his own, and as an independent observer, would provide strong testimony for Mogollon distinctiveness. Because Morris was occupied with his own Basketmaker sites near Durango, however, Haury tackled the problem himself. He began his first field school in the Forestdale Valley in the summer of 1939.

Soon other archaeologists joined the Mogollon fray. In 1939, Martin and Rinaldo began their long-term investigations of the Mogollon in the Pine Lawn–Reserve region of west-central New Mexico, a locale we suspect was chosen after reviewing the Gila Pueblo records of the 1931 Haury-Hastings "survey of discovery." Erik K. Reed, who by age nineteen had completed all requirements for a Harvard PhD except a dissertation, had become a Mogollon advocate through his fieldwork at the Harris Village (and perhaps also through his work as a member of the 1934–35 Snaketown crew). At the time, Reed was probably working on the first of two dissertation drafts synthesizing what was known of Southwest prehistory. Although both were rejected by his committee, he would use them as a source of major journal articles published throughout the 1940s that defended the Mogollon concept.

By 1939, the major questions concerning the Mogollon had been voiced, and the participants in the debate had aligned themselves—Kidder, Brew, and Harvard University against the transplanted southwesterners, Haury, Reed, Martin, and Rinaldo. Earlier, around the turn of the twentieth century, Southwest archaeologists had struggled to protect their archaeological resources from collecting and removal by outsiders from the elite institutions of the East Coast (Snead 2001). Perhaps the dichotomy

lingered still in the alignments of the Mogollon controversy. Other archaeologists, primarily students, would join the discussion, and Kidder would
switch sides, but these would be the major players in the Mogollon controversy for the next two decades. The opening salvo in Haury's program
to validate the Mogollon concept took place in the Forestdale Valley of
Arizona. We take our story there next.

7
Forestdale Valley, Arizona

The physical discreteness of the valley was one of the qualities
that attracted us to it, for the archaeological problems could
thereby be more easily contained, and we foresaw the possibility
of developing a notion of valley prehistory in the time and
with the resources available to us.

—Emil Haury (1985a:13)

As head of the Anthropology Department and director of the Arizona
State Museum, Haury was in a position to give expression to his established research interests in the Hohokam of the desert and the Mogollon
of the mountains. He knew that the Arizona desert was not a congenial
environment for fieldwork during the summer, the period of maximum
field activity for university archaeologists. During the school year, therefore, he mounted his Papaguería project within striking distance of the
university (Reid 2008). The most important contribution of this project
was the excavation of Ventana Cave, a rockshelter with stratified deposits
spanning the Archaic period, perhaps even earlier, through the Historic
period (Haury 1950a).

To investigate the Mogollon, Haury took the summer field school to
the high country of east-central Arizona—the Forestdale Valley just below
the Mogollon Rim on the Fort Apache Reservation. Haury's stated purpose was research into the prehistory of the Forestdale Valley as it bore
directly on the mounting controversy over his concept of the Mogollon
Culture. He wrote:

One of the currently debated questions in southwestern archaeology
concerns the identification, if not the reality, of the Mogollon Culture. It was the intention of the Arizona State Museum and the Department of Anthropology at the University of Arizona to bring new

evidence to bear on this problem when, in 1939, investigations were begun in the Forestdale Valley, Fort Apache Indian Reservation, Arizona. (Haury 1985a:285)

With subtle skill, Haury would maneuver his field schools at Forestdale (1939–41) and later at Point of Pines (1946–60) to validate the Mogollon concept. The Mogollon problem gave an immediate research purpose to the field school while simultaneously embroiling it in controversy from the beginning. The field schools of 1939, 1940, and 1941 combined students and Apache workmen in the pursuit of Haury's research goals, and he sought to enhance the impact of the research through conferences and invitations that brought prominent archaeologists to view the record firsthand.

Forestdale Valley

The Forestdale Valley is something akin to a secret garden—a narrow, mountain valley nestled just below the Mogollon Rim (see fig. 4.2). Hills deep with ponderosa pine, juniper, oak, and manzanita enclose it. In summer, the valley is impossibly green, rich with grass and wildflowers brought by the summer thunderstorms, punctuated here and there with the deeper green of juniper and the white blooms of thistle poppy. Forestdale Creek, which in ancient times probably was a perennial stream, wanders through the valley. Walnut, willow, and other riparian vegetation hugs the creek banks. More than twenty inches of rainfall drench the land, and numerous springs along the valley margin form pockets of luxuriant vegetation. Water and good alluvial bottom land made this little valley an attractive locale for settlement—first by the Mogollon, then by the Western Apache, and finally by Mormon and Gentile farmers who grew potatoes, corn, beans, and squash. Today, tumbledown wooden cabins grayed by time testify to the latest farmers' short time in the valley.

Haury had initially surveyed the Forestdale Valley in 1931 as part of his mountain reconnaissance with Hastings for Gila Pueblo. He knew it to be rich with a variety of sites, some of which had the brown pottery characteristic of the Mogollon tradition. He also thought it important to excavate a site located near the northern limits of the Mogollon culture's distribution for two reasons. "First, being in juxtaposition to Basketmaker, it was supposed that the likes and unlikes and the degree of amalgamation between the two could be picked up easily; second, that if no amalgamation was indicated, the contrast between the Basketmaker and Mogollon would be all the greater in view of the frontier location" (Haury 1985a:140).

With the promise of six hours of academic credit for eight weeks of fieldwork, Haury easily assembled an eager group of students. Tents were purchased, and the university provided cots. Brew lent the enormous, direct-current generator that had provided electricity for the field camp at Awat'ovi. Haury recalled they selected a green, grassy spot at the foot of a hill for the camp site, and piped water from a spring of cold, sweet water into the kitchen tent, where the cook, Sarge Brown, turned out regular and hearty meals for the hungry crew.

Bear Village

Bear Village, named for a black cub that was captured and became the camp mascot, was the first site Haury excavated. There, Haury (1940, 1985a) defined a pit-house occupation dating between the late AD 600s and the AD 800s, contemporary with major occupations of the Mogollon and Harris villages. Bear Village lies on the valley floor near Forestdale Creek, with its pit houses dug deep into the alluvial clays. The crew excavated seventeen houses, about half of the total present, and a strangely shaped great kiva. Although three excavated houses were rectangular, most were round, and all exhibited mixed architectural features characteristic of the Mogollon and Anasazi. The Anasazi traits included benches around the house perimeter, four-post roof-support systems, hearths with clay rims, ventilators, and floor ridges; the Mogollon houses lacked these architectural features. Inside habitation structures were cooking hearths, food-processing equipment, and storage pits in higher frequency than in the two excavated storage rooms.

The great kiva was shaped like a quadruped creature resembling a turtle. Recesses suggestive of legs were located at the cardinal directions, and a larger, rounder recessed area resembled the head. Haury was inclined to believe these characteristics were functional, and the effigy resemblance was coincidental. Ladder holes near the hearth suggested that the kiva was entered through the roof. A trench in the floor may have served as a foot drum.

Animal remains indicated substantial hunting of deer, whereas milling equipment was certain evidence for processing plant foods. Although only one charred corn cob was recovered in an era before adequate techniques for retrieving botanical remains had been developed, it is reasonable to infer that corn was a significant component of the diet, although we doubt that they were dependent on farming. The short growing season (134 days) and killing frosts through May offset the valley's rich soil and ample water.

The plain ware pottery so closely resembled that of the Mimbres and San Francisco river valleys that Haury did not define a new type. In addition to Alma Plain, the assemblage included Forestdale Smudged, a thin, fine-paste ware with deep-black, lustrous interiors; Forestdale Red, an unslipped red ware similar to San Francisco Red; and Forestdale Plain, which Haury described as representing a fusion of Anasazi and Mogollon technology.

The significance of the Bear Village to the Mogollon problem was twofold. First, it corroborated the antiquity claimed for the Mogollon and Harris villages with additional tree-ring dates. Haury noted the probable development of the Mogollon culture from preceramic Cochise culture roots, a notion that Sayles and Antevs (1941) shortly would present in print, and he forwarded the notion that the Mogollon culture was roughly comparable to the Archaic period of Mexico in that it was "the underpinning for the later and higher cultural groups" (Haury 1940:131).

Second, the Bear report demonstrated that the Mogollon traits found in the Mimbres and San Francisco river valleys of New Mexico were not aberrant, but also extended into the mountains of east-central Arizona. Haury, of course, had seen the surface evidence of this widespread geographic distribution of similar remains back in 1931, but excavation data added considerable weight to the argument. Furthermore, according to Haury, although Bear Village was distinctive in many material remains, it also displayed some Anasazi traits, which Haury interpreted as amalgamation of cultural characteristics. Many years later, this mixing of characteristics would be reinterpreted as indicating ethnic coresidence of Mogollon and Anasazi households (Reid 1989:72–73). Last, Haury predicted an earlier phase would precede the Georgetown and Forestdale phases. Paul Sidney Martin would discover this at the SU site in New Mexico, and Haury himself would uncover evidence for it at Bluff Village.

Bluff Village

In 1941, the last summer of the field school at Forestdale, Haury began excavation at the Bluff site. This pit-house village produced strong evidence for plain brown pottery and pit houses that were tree-ring dated to around AD 300. After a two-year hiatus, the excavation was completed during the summer of 1944 (Haury and Sayles 1947; Haury 1985a).

The site, located about a mile and half from Bear Village, was named for the bluff of Coconino sandstone on which it sits, requiring a brief but breathless hike up from the valley floor to a commanding view. The scarcity of ceramics and the resemblance of the few sherds they found to Apache pottery had convinced Haury and crew that the Bluff site was an Apache encampment. What they encountered, however, was evidence for the earliest Mogollon occupation in Arizona.

The archaeologists uncovered twenty-three pit houses, an estimated two-thirds of those originally present. They ranged in shape from circular and oval to square with rounded corners; this, and their apparently random location across the site surface, indicated repeated, multiple occupations over a long time. Pottery was not plentiful and was almost exclusively brown plain ware. During the earliest-dated occupation, circular pit houses were dug into the fractured bedrock of the bluff. The larger houses contained hearths, suggesting their use for habitation, and the size of Structure 5 (83 m^2) led Haury to propose it had communal and possibly religious functions in addition to habitation. Subsequent occupation by people who built the oval houses and later the square houses indicated a continuing preference for this bluff-top location with its panoramic view of the valley floor.

The immediate significance of Bluff Village to the Mogollon controversy was in the tree-ring dates, which were discussed in 1942 in a small but critical paper (reprinted in Haury 1985a) before the excavation had been completed. A graduate student who had worked at Bluff Village had carried out a preliminary analysis of the samples during a class on dendrochronology at the University of Arizona, coming up with a date around AD 310 on about twenty specimens. At Haury's request, perhaps to head off any criticism of the interpretations based on analytical expertise, Douglass reanalyzed the tree-ring specimens and prepared a report verifying and sustaining the original dates (Douglass 1985). Dates were obtained from nine, possibly ten, different trees, including two with cutting dates, from six different houses. Haury's conclusion was characteristically terse:

> [The] 4th century date from the Bluff Site would appear to give us the earliest ruin with a pottery complement yet dated by tree-rings. Ever since considerable age has been claimed for the Mogollon Culture and

particularly the proposal that Mogollon pottery may have been in existence before Anasazi ceramics, the lack of tree-ring dates has been cited as the central argument against it. While the evidence from the Bluff Site is still not conclusive it is nevertheless in support of this line of reasoning. (Haury 1985a:442)

In the "Recapitulation" section that ended the Bluff report, Haury listed in his typical format the traits that placed the site firmly in the Mogollon camp and supported the argument for the temporal priority of Mogollon ceramics over Anasazi pottery. Bluff Village firmly situated the Mogollon alongside Anasazi and Hohokam as one of the basic cultures of the American Southwest, one with its roots planted in the local population of the preceramic era.

Tla Kii Pueblo

The Forestdale Valley provided additional evidence to convince Haury that his original postulation of amalgamation was correct—that the Anasazi assimilated the Mogollon and submerged the distinctive Mogollon traits. In 1940 and 1941, the field school excavated Tla Kii Pueblo, a small ruin of twenty-one habitation and storage rooms, a detached small kiva, and a large, circular great kiva. Tree-ring dates placed the occupation of the pueblo between AD 1100 and 1150. Tla Kii stands out as an example of life in a small pueblo community that owed much of its architectural character to an Anasazi tradition. Utility pottery, however, included the ubiquitous brown ware, both plain and corrugated, along with red-slipped vessels and others with smudged interiors, all common features of mountain pottery for hundreds of years. Decorated pottery included white-painted corrugated ware, another well-established mountain tradition, and black-on-red and black-on-white painted pottery of indisputable Anasazi origin.

Tla Kii Pueblo represented a small, agricultural community with corn fields on the valley floor. Hunting and gathering continued to provide a goodly portion of the diet. Even though the degree of Anasazi assimilation may still be debated, contact and exchange between groups of Mogollon and Anasazi, as well as coresidence, can be seen in architecture, pottery, and mortuary practices. The presence of a great kiva, in addition to a small kiva, suggests activities involving more people than those who inhabited the twenty-one-room pueblo.

The Tla Kii report was not published until 1985 (Haury 1985a), in large part, we think, because it did not play a critical role in the argument to validate the separateness or antiquity of the Mogollon as well as because Haury's increasing administrative duties left little time for writing. Recognized as the first pueblo village in the Forestdale Valley, Tla Kii was followed by Forestdale Pueblo (AZ P:16:9 in the Arizona State Museum system), occupied in the late AD 1200s, and the large pueblo ruin of Tundastusa, which was occupied in the AD 1300s. The transition from pit-house villages to masonry pueblos in this small mountain valley served to convince Haury of the correctness of his interpretation of Mogollon assimilation and submergence sometime around AD 1000, and to our knowledge, he never changed his mind on this point (see Haury 1985a:403–7).

Taking the Mogollon Controversy Beyond the Forestdale Valley

The Forestdale work addressed and answered with the hard evidence of excavation the major objections to Haury's original definition of the Mogollon culture. Its authenticity had been demonstrated by documenting a set of traits over a broad geographic range extending from the Mimbres and San Francisco river valleys of New Mexico to the Forestdale Valley of east-central Arizona. Its antiquity had been established by the tree-ring dates from the Bluff Village. Forestdale also supported the notion of assimilation.

After the field schools in the Forestdale Valley ended, Haury continued to defend the Mogollon concept directly and indirectly through a wide range of publications. His 1943 paper on "A Possible Cochise-Mogollon-Hohokam Sequence" proceeded from observations he had made concerning the Cochise connection. Citing data from his work at Mogollon and Harris villages and in the Forestdale Valley, along with Martin's research at the SU site in New Mexico, Haury concluded that "the addition of pottery, agriculture and a few other traits to the lithic industry of the San Pedro stage, seems to have ushered in the earliest Mogollon horizon" (Haury 1943:261). San Pedro was the latest stage of the preceramic (Archaic) Cochise culture of southeastern Arizona, which had been defined by Gila Pueblo archaeologists (Sayles and Antevs 1941).

In 1945, Haury authored two publications bearing indirectly upon the Mogollon problem. One concerned Los Muertos, the subject of Haury's

1934 dissertation at Harvard, which was published as a Peabody Museum paper in 1945. Although focusing on Hohokam, Haury presented the Mogollon connection through the Salado culture, which he viewed as having developed in the area below the Mogollon Rim out of a "combined Mogollon-Anasazi base—stamped most heavily by the latter" (Haury 1945a:205). Here and in "The Problems of Contacts Between Mexico and the Southwestern United States" (Haury 1945b) Haury reiterated his interpretation that the Mogollon had lost identity during the closing centuries of the first millennium AD.

Why, then, did the Mogollon controversy persist? Our first response to this question is that scholars and institutions voiced strong opinions and claimed ideological positions during a time when all attention was being directed toward the sacrifices and demands of World War II. Clearly, the war halted much archaeological work, as it did with the cessation of the Forestdale field school, but it also deflected attention away from normal modes of academic discourse and impeded personal interaction. Other observers might interpret the "fog of war" as being nothing more than a moratorium on nonessential activities during wartime. There is truth in both views.

In a "state of the art" article, Neil M. Judd, nephew of Cummings and a prominent archaeologist who worked in Chaco Canyon, New Mexico, set the wartime tone for the anti-Mogollon faction when he wrote (1940:433), "the Mogollon appears to be an illegitimate whose paternity is still under scrutiny." The publication that might have been seen as resolving the paternity suit in actuality only served to heighten antagonism to the Mogollon. This was John C. McGregor's 1941 textbook *Southwestern Archaeology* (1941a), the first book-length synthesis to appear since Kidder's *An Introduction to the Study of Southwestern Archaeology* of 1924. With this publication, McGregor created and unleashed a Mogollon whirlwind. Where others equivocated, McGregor promoted unequivocally.

McGregor received his master's degree from the University of Arizona, where he worked at Hohokam sites in the vicinity of Tucson. Haury introduced him to the archaeology of the Four Corners region on a momentous expedition in 1927, the details of which, as described in McGregor's (1987) autobiography, can only be seen as harrowing. In 1930, McGregor was hired as a curator of archaeology at the Museum of Northern Arizona. He credited his experience in tree-ring dating with Douglass at the University of Arizona as being instrumental in obtaining this position. While at the museum, McGregor worked at many different sites in the

Flagstaff area. These experiences, and his encounters with the vast variety of terrain in Arizona, no doubt shaped his view of the state's ancient cultures.

In his book, McGregor catapulted the Mogollon from its position as a peripheral, borrowing variant of Anasazi into the central culture from which virtually everything else in the Southwest developed. He accepted that Mogollon developed from a preceramic, Cochise culture base and therefore was early. As such, Mogollon was a "basic culture," one of two in the Southwest. One gave rise to Hohokam, Mogollon, and possibly Patayan, and the other formed Basketmaker-Pueblo. In McGregor's view, Mogollon was probably the earliest highly developed and distinctive culture in Arizona and in this capacity, influenced Basketmaker by being responsible for the introduction of pottery and architecture. In fact, McGregor proposed that a cross between Mogollon and Basketmaker produced the Pueblo culture. Anasazi was a label with geographical utility only. McGregor saw no difficulty in having the Pueblo return around AD 1000 to assimilate the Mogollon.

In addition to this textbook synthesis, McGregor reported in 1941 on his excavations at Winona and Ridge Ruin (1941b), sites a little more than ten miles east of Flagstaff, Arizona. In this work, the Mogollon were credited with contributing a larger part to the Sinagua culture of the Flagstaff area than did the Anasazi, the latter offering only surface masonry and a lot of trade pottery. Mogollon exceeded mere distinctiveness as a culture by acquiring the role of agent in cultural influence and change. McGregor's bold claims would fuel the controversy to a new level of intensity by providing the spark igniting the most vociferous attacks yet upon the Mogollon.

Although Gila Pueblo never recovered from Haury's departure in 1937, Gladwin continued to publish new, revised interpretations of Southwest prehistory. In his 1942 revision of the original 1937 Snaketown report, he devoted much attention to the Mogollon problem. By that time, Gladwin had come to believe there was no Mogollon, only cultures descended from and showing varying degrees of influence from a more pervasive complex, which he dubbed Cordilleran. The Mogollon continued to suffer revision and modification in Gladwin's efforts to shorten the Hohokam chronology, with the net effect of being more of an irritant to Haury personally than a substantive contribution to academic discourse. For example, in 1948, Gladwin authored one of his most radical reinterpretations. He reanalyzed the stratigraphy of Mound 29 at Snaketown—the foundation for Haury's Hohokam chronology and phase sequence—and completely revised the chronology on this basis. He compressed the entire span of occupation at Snaketown to two phases covering less than four hundred years. To make this feat seem plausible, Gladwin proposed the presence of two different peoples at Snaketown—the Hohokam and Mogollon. The Mogollon were responsible for the pottery types representing the Pioneer period. To accomplish all of this, it was necessary for Gladwin to revise upward the Mogollon chronology and associated ceramic development. His revision of Hohokam, therefore, was predicated on doing the same for the Mogollon.

In chasing an answer to why there was a Mogollon controversy after Haury's reports on the Forestdale Valley discoveries, we have gotten a little ahead of our story and perhaps even given the impression that Haury was alone and there really was not much of a controversy at all. In point of fact, he had several highly capable and extremely active supporters, though not all agreed on every feature of Mogollon interpretation. Throughout the 1940s, Martin and Rinaldo were busily compiling the hard evidence of excavation from their field station in the Pine Lawn Valley of western New Mexico, and Reed was publishing provocative papers that were leading to a confirmation, but also a redefinition, of Mogollon. In 1946, Haury transferred the field school to Point of Pines on the San Carlos Apache Reservation. Subsequent chapters will position the thoughts and activities of these pro-Mogollonists as layers to the mounting controversy of the 1940s. First, however, we must turn to Brew and his opposition to all things Mogollon. This story takes us to the windswept mesas of Hopi land and the sagebrush country of Colorado.

8

Alkali Ridge, Awat'ovi, and the Anasazi Frontier

> The question is, do we wish to find out what happened in
> the past and why it happened, or do we, like the Dictators
> of the present day, wish to jam our beliefs down other
> peoples' throats.
>
> —John Otis Brew (1946:75)

J. O. Brew was arguably the most provocative and vehement antagonist
to the Mogollon concept. Like Haury, he was the product of a Harvard
University education, and he would go on to a distinguished career at that
institution. Brew's opening attack in the controversy was his review of
McGregor's textbook *Southwestern Archaeology* in *American Antiquity*
(Brew 1942), and it is one of the strongest reviews that we have ever read.
With its harsh criticisms of the Mogollon culture, this review established
Brew as the major opponent to the Mogollon concept, a position he would
retain for decades (Wendorf 2008:64).

Much of the antagonism voiced in this review was bound up with the
other disagreements Brew had with McGregor's work, making it difficult
to tease out the Mogollon-specific threads of the argument. A few statements from the long and thorough review should make this point clear:

> Students have long looked forward to Dr. McGregor's book. The tes-
> timony here presented, on the basis of the most careful reading I
> have ever given a text book, is the opinion that this book does not fill
> our need. It is a great disappointment. (Brew 1942:191)

> Dr. McGregor's book is presented as a textbook for beginners. Actually,
> it can be read without serious danger only by those who are thoroughly
> familiar with all aspects of Southwestern archaeology. (Brew 1942:192)

McGregor's book is not only unscientific, in the terms described above, but it is expressed in a dogmatic style, startling and anachronistic in the year 1942. (Brew 1942:192)

Unfortunately there are many other points to which exception can and will be taken. I shall list no more of them. For, after all, the main difficulty with this book does not lie in these specific items. Its glaring fault is the continuous bald statement of *one hypothesis only* [emphasis in original]in highly controversial matters. These statements are usually clothed in such positive terms that unwary students are given no indication that they are not dealing with established and demonstrable fact. "Theirs not to reason why. . . ." (Brew 1942:196)

Brew's criticisms more specifically directed to the Mogollon include McGregor's attempts to establish Mogollon as a "basic culture" in the absence of what Brew would consider sufficient evidence. He noted the lack of distinctive traits and that in the list of Mogollon traits, "there is not one which does not occur also in either Pueblo or Hohokam or both" (Brew 1942:193). Moreover, he emphasized McGregor's own statement that all Mogollon sites excavated at that time were outside its geographical center and therefore could well be atypical. He found unacceptable the assertion that Mogollon influenced other cultures and was critical of the dating, especially its extension back to AD 1. To Brew, the distinctiveness and antiquity of Mogollon as well as its affinity with the preceramic Cochise culture were still unproven. The only statement McGregor made concerning Mogollon that Brew was willing to accept was that the Mogollon culture was poorly known.

For reasons not apparent in the published literature, Brew seems inadvertently to have backed himself into a corner on the Mogollon issue while criticizing justifiably the looseness of McGregor's reconstructions. On the one hand, Brew called for more rigor in archaeological thought, especially taxonomy, while on the other hand, he dismissed as insubstantial the evidence in support of the Mogollon as a "basic culture," although the evidential requirements of a "basic culture" were left vague. Nonetheless, Brew's comments added a critical, new dimension to the controversy—concern with a rigorous definition and use of terms—that we think is a direct reflection of the atmosphere of archaeological thought then prevailing at Harvard. Perhaps in response to these issues, Reed's papers that appeared throughout the 1940s took evidence, tradition, and definition as their central themes, and by the end of the decade, this work resulted in an expanded concept of the Mogollon culture.

It is annoying that we have been unable to locate a published response by McGregor to Brew's scathing review. McGregor's (1987) unpublished, three-hundred-page memoir does not even mention his 1941 edition of *Southwestern Archaeology* or the 1965 republication of the reorganized book, which changed cultures to periods, much less the furor created by the original publication. In fact, he wrote in the short preface to his unpublished memoirs that "These have been enjoyable years, and my memory of them is now most pleasant, for I have found that one forgets unpleasantries and remembers only those happy events which over the years have grown to be even more enjoyable." Because some elderly men become mellow as well as forgetful, we found it necessary to search the archives for answers.

On November 4, 1942, McGregor wrote to Frank H. H. Roberts Jr., another illustrious archaeologist of the Bureau of American Ethnology, acknowledging his review of McGregor's report on the sites of Winona and Ridge Ruin. He also wrote to Brew regarding his review of *Southwestern Archaeology*: "Dear Joe: I have just read with the greatest of interest your critical review in [American] ANTIQUITY of the SOUTHWESTERN ARCHAEOLOGY. From it I can see that there are points which we will have to discuss sometime together, but not in the pages of [American] ANTIQUITY."

A letter to Haury dated November 23, 1942, is more revealing. In it, McGregor wrote: "The Mogollon situation is as we both know a real and important one. This was the main grounds of complaint in the Brew review of my text; otherwise he had little to say. Incidentally I was annoyed only by the way in which he criticized this book, not by the fact that he criticized it, and therefore agree with you that some of his criticisms were justifiable."

Two weeks later in a letter to Gladwin dated December 8, 1942, McGregor gave us a little more of his reaction: "The violent criticisms by J. O. Brew of my Southwestern Archaeology, so far as I can see, are based only on his refusal to admit the existence of Mogollon and its influence in the development of Pueblo. I wonder if he will even admit Cochise? This is such a vital subject just now that you [Gladwin], with your insight into it and your data bearing on it, could go far in straightening out a badly muddled mess. I for one wish you could get your hat into this particular ring just now, too." Gladwin, however, in contrast to Brew, would only add to the "muddled mess" that was Mogollon.

John Otis Brew of the Peabody Museum, Harvard University

Who was John Otis (Jo) Brew (fig. 8.1), the bête noire of Mogollon archaeologists? We never had the opportunity to interview him, although he stopped by the University of Arizona once on a visit to the family of his son Lindsay, a Tucson lawyer. Afterward, he sent a postcard dated October 16, 1979, reading: "Dear Jeff, Under separate cover I am sending you a book containing my 'obituary.' It still does not tell you my private thoughts about my colleagues, but it may amuse you. Sincerely, Jo Brew." Those unrecorded private thoughts must be pieced together from other sources.

Figure 8.1 John Otis (Jo) Brew, director of the Peabody Museum, Harvard University, at Point of Pines in 1948. (Photograph by Phil Hobler; courtesy of the Arizona State Museum; neg. no. 7879)

The book Brew sent is Walter Muir Whitehill's *Analecta Biographica: A Handful of New England Portraits* (1969), wherein chapter 17 contains a collection of congratulatory statements by longtime Brew friends and colleagues Richard Woodbury, Edward Danson, H. M. Wormington, Richard Daugherty, and Emil Haury. Haury's comments, written in the late 1960s, laud Brew's achievements during what Woodbury (1990) would later chronicle as Brew's third career, promoting salvage archaeology and international heritage preservation:

> By emphasizing the foregoing aspect [salvage archaeology] of Jo's career, his capabilities as an archaeologist and a scholar are not being minimized. He had made valuable and significant contributions in his own right to American archaeology, both through his own writing and in providing opportunities for others to go into the field to conduct research and to publish. That latter aspect is eventually the fate of the administrator and most of the time those efforts go unsung. (Haury, in Whitehill 1969:216–17)

Even if we credit the mellowness that age sometimes confers, this passage holds no hint of discord between Haury—definer and defender of the Mogollon—and Brew, its most prominent opponent and adversarial strategist. Brew questioned the intellectual merit of the Mogollon concept from the vantage of one who had devoted most of the 1930s to filling in gaps in the Anasazi developmental sequence that Kidder had sketched at Pecos in 1927. Effectively, Brew was the heir apparent to the Kidder legacy of upholding high standards of culture-historical interpretation based on extensive archaeological fieldwork. Above all, he enjoyed intellectual arguments for their own sake.

Born March 28, 1906, Brew was only two years younger than Haury, yet his hometown of Malden, Massachusetts, was about as distant, socially and geographically, as one could get from Newton, Kansas. Brew died in Cambridge, Massachusetts, in 1988, four years before Haury. Of Woodbury's (1990) three Brews—archaeologist, administrator, and salvage-archaeology promoter—only the first two are critical to our Mogollon story. Having completed his residence requirements at Harvard in 1931, he joined the Peabody Museum's Claflin-Emerson Expedition to Utah, the same summer that Haury and Hastings surveyed the mountains of Arizona and New Mexico. In the fall of that year, Brew directed the Museum's Southeastern Utah Expedition to Alkali Ridge, where he conducted two additional, lengthy seasons of fieldwork. His report, published in 1946, laid the foundation for understanding the Pueblo I period in the Anasazi region. It also addressed several methodological issues perplexing archaeologists of the 1930s.

Brew's second major archaeological field project was directing the Peabody Museum's Awat'ovi Expedition from 1936 to 1939. Awat'ovi, a prehistoric and historical-period Hopi village on the edge of Antelope Mesa overlooking the Jeddito Valley, is only tangentially relevant to our Mogollon story, though its own history is immensely fascinating. It may have been the first Hopi village that Vasquez de Coronado's officer, Pedro de Tovar, encountered in the summer of 1540, and it was certainly the village razed in the winter of 1700–1701 in retribution for its reacceptance of Spanish clerics.

Under Brew's direction, the Awat'ovi Expedition excavated 21 sites and located 275 others on Antelope Mesa and in the Jeddito Valley. About 1,300 rooms and kivas were excavated at Awat'ovi and 200 more at the other sites, which included the famed kiva murals of Kawaika'a and the pit houses of Jeddito 264. Hiroshi Daifuku's (1961) dissertation on Jeddito 264, completed in 1950, would take as its major premise that the Mogollon culture was simply a regional variant of Pueblo Anasazi.

Perhaps as early as the late 1930s and surely by the early 1940s, Brew was an acknowledged Anasazi authority, Kidder having left active research a decade earlier to direct the Carnegie Institution's work in Mesoamerica. Brew held a commanding position as assistant curator of southwestern archaeology (1941) and later (1945) as curator of North American archaeology at the Harvard Peabody Museum. It was from this vantage that he reviewed McGregor's *Southwestern Archaeology*.

In 1946, Brew ventured further into the Mogollon fray with his 1946 Alkali Ridge report. It was, in part, a documentation of his disbelief in Mogollon distinctiveness and antiquity. We spend some time with the report, because it articulated more clearly than any other contemporary work the criticisms levied against the Mogollon culture and because of Brew's own eminence in the discipline, which surely must have influenced his colleagues.

Alkali Ridge

Alkali Ridge is located in the middle reaches of the San Juan River, at that time arguably the center of the southwestern universe. It straddles a ridge between Alkali Canyon and tributaries of Montezuma Canyon, south of Monticello, Utah, and in the shadow of the Abajo, or Blue, Mountains. Brew's (1946:13) arid description of the environment belies its deep allure: "The landscape is characterized by small evergreen trees, pinyon and juniper, and sagebrush." His words do not hint at the indescribable scent of sage standing taller than a person in the canyon bottoms, or the layered ruggedness of the canyons cutting through the earth, or the oddly comforting bulk of the Blues, hazy in the distance. Culturally, geographically, and intellectually, the archaeology of Alkali Ridge was the polar opposite of that surrounding the fledgling Mogollon culture, far from the Colorado Plateau heartland of Southwest archaeology and defended by archaeologists from homegrown institutions.

Brew (1946:44–66) set the stage for the critique of the Mogollon concept in his oft-quoted essay on "The Use and Abuse of Taxonomy." In this chapter, he surveyed the status of cultural-historical classification at that time and advanced the notions that classification is not an end in itself but a means to an end, and classificatory systems require a conceptual scheme if they are to be useful. This discussion brought Brew to the hinge point: how to place a trait, a group of traits, a site, or part of a site into a taxonomic scheme. Citing Clyde Kluckhohn, the eminent anthropologist we will meet shortly, Brew observed the tyranny of the variation from the norm, which requires the archaeologist to force the data into existing systems or create new ones.

Having set the scene for the reader, Brew (1946:74–85) held up the Mogollon concept as an example in "The Present Situation," citing its significance in the minds of southwestern archaeologists, the fact that it impinged upon most of the important problems in Anasazi archaeology, and because it seemed to be "the most unstable and least definite of the Southwestern 'cultures'" (Brew 1946:75). Because of that instability, he wrote (Brew 1946:750), "the history of its general adoption provides splendid illustrations of some of the procedures I think should be guarded against, particularly the undue haste exhibited by students in general in snatching at a new panacea before its nature and properties are known even by those who have produced it."

Brew first criticized the dating of Mogollon, emphasizing that the Snaketown chronology could not be used to validate early Mogollon dates because the Snaketown chronology itself was questionable. Brew lamented the absence of absolute dating and mentioned the Bluff Village tree-ring dates only in a footnote.

Brew also devoted considerable attention to the lack of distinctiveness in Mogollon architecture, stone artifacts, and pottery. Some of these criticisms appear biased; for example, he pointed out the variability in the Bear Village architecture as support for the lack-of-distinctiveness argument, when Haury had stressed throughout the report that Mogollon and Anasazi traits merged at that site. Brew was willing to concede that the facilities Haury labeled "cooking pits" (roasting pits) did separate the Mogollon from their neighbors and possibly represented "some specialized culinary or industrial practice" (Brew 1946:80). He also observed that the polished red ware of the Mogollon region lay behind the cultural construct and was the strongest support for its distinctiveness, although he also noted that red ware was not restricted to the Mogollon but might have its origins in ancient Mexico. (Brew's notion was not too far off the mark; much later, archaeologists would point to a broadly distributed, early ceramic horizon embracing the Southwest and northern Mexico from which later regional ceramic traditions arose [see Whittlesey 2004b].)

Brew (1946:79) concluded that "the concept of Mogollon culture is far from being established as an aggregation of a sufficient number of cultural traits to permit us to consider it on a par with Hohokam and Pueblo." In support of this position, Brew cited Alfred Kroeber, the influential, Columbia University–educated cultural anthropologist of Berkeley; Kidder; and Nesbitt as authorities who shared his skepticism. He also stated repeatedly that Haury shared that skepticism to some degree—he "has never considered it to be satisfactorily established and is devoting himself to the study of its validity as a basic culture." In contrast to Haury's stance, "The whole-hearted acceptance of the Mogollon has been by others, workers for the most part outside of the central Mogollon area, and university teachers who have grasped it, uncritically, as a welcome and easy solution to many of the problems of the origin and diffusion of traits in the Pueblo and the Hohokam" (Brew 1946:79). In this jibe, he probably meant Paul Sidney Martin and John McGregor.

The crux of the matter and the probable reason for Brew's disdain for the Mogollon concept and its characteristic polished red ware was Abajo Red-on-orange, a puzzling pottery type that was found in quantity at Alkali Ridge. The Peabody Museum Southeastern Utah Expedition had discovered that the earliest painted pottery on Alkali Ridge was a bichrome ware decorated with red mineral paint on an unslipped, orange background. Martin and Morris had found this pottery in Colorado, and Brew (1946:83) indicated it also was present in Chaco Canyon. Martin and Rinaldo (1940:10) had written that this ware, first thought to be an independent invention of the local Basketmaker people, actually was somehow related to Mogollon red-on-brown wares, a connection that Haury had previously recognized. Nothing was more certain to raise hackles among Anasazi archaeologists; it was the archaeological equivalent of cheating at cards. Brew did his best to discredit the resemblance between Mogollon painted pottery and Abajo Red-on-orange, but his arguments ring hollow. Most striking was his observation that Abajo Red-on-orange closely resembled Dragoon Red-on-brown ceramics, an early, broad-line-painted type found at sites excavated by the Amerind Foundation near Dragoon in southeastern Arizona, and both painted types bore designs similar to San Juan Basketmaker II and III baskets (Brew 1946:84). Some archaeologists now conceive the Dragoon wares as part of an indigenous ceramic tradition with strong Mogollon roots (Heckman, Montgomery, and Whittlesey 2000; Whittlesey 2004b).

Without doubt, Alkali Ridge is an excellent report of well-executed archaeological excavations and a thoughtful consideration of some methodological excesses then current in American archaeology. Only the discussion of the Mogollon was peculiarly out of date, having been composed around 1940 and little altered for publication six years later, perhaps because of the pressure of Brew's growing administrative responsibilities, for he became director of the Peabody Museum in 1948. The impact upon the Mogollon controversy was that an essentially outmoded argument would be perpetuated through the 1940s and beyond on the weight of Brew's influence, authority, and institutional power. To his lasting credit, however, Brew's third and last major field project would put him, his close colleagues, and his Harvard students on the front line of the Mogollon controversy.

Like Haury, Brew knew that archaeological arguments are resolved through fieldwork. After the war, he and Donald Scott, at that time director of the Peabody, initiated a project they had conceived in the 1930s. The Peabody Museum's Upper Gila Expedition explored a region of west-central New Mexico that was geographically intermediate between the Anasazi and Mogollon culture areas. A brief comment documents that the project was designed to elucidate the Mogollon controversy: an "enigmatic Mogollon culture is postulated as an intriguing prospect as yet not supported with a sufficient number of distinct traits to give it acceptable validity as a useful concept in our historical reconstructions" (Brew and Danson 1948:211–22). The Upper Gila Expedition was conducted between 1949, the year that Brew was named Peabody Professor of American archaeology, succeeding Scott, and 1954. It produced two major contributions to the Mogollon controversy—the reports by Danson (1957) and Bullard (1962). This work would amass a large database of Mogollon sites in west-central New Mexico, information that would support claims for Mogollon distinctiveness and put to rest any notion that such claims were based on inadequate data. Unfortunately, by the time the reports were published, the controversy had largely diminished.

It is worth spending a moment examining Haury's reaction to Brew's Alkali Ridge report. In 1949, Haury reviewed the book for *American Antiquity*. Haury opened the critique with the statement that "*The Archaeology of Alkali Ridge, Southeastern Utah* is, beyond doubt, one of the best written, most complete, and thought-provoking additions to the literature on American prehistory" (Haury 1949b:64). He then goes on to dismantle Brew's notions about biological taxonomy as applied to archaeology, arming himself with excerpts from a memorandum written by a colleague in biology, Dr. Charles Reed. Next, Haury (1949b:65) stated that "*Alkali Ridge* is so packed full of all manner of problems which are subject to review that it becomes difficult to choose between them." But choose he did, and his choice not surprisingly was a few further comments on the Mogollon culture. Haury (1949b:65–66) criticized Brew's notion that the Mogollon had an insufficient number of traits to be recognized as a "basic culture": "In fact we shall, in all probability, have many fewer traits by which Mogollon may be characterized than are available for the other groups even after years of work because of the very nature of the culture." Haury also refuted Brew's contention that the number of Mogollon sites was small; there were as many Mogollon site reports as Basketmaker site reports, if not more. Haury (1949b:66) concluded wryly by expressing his deep curiosity concerning how Brew would "attack certain cultural problems which are bound to arise in the course of the Peabody Museum's Upper Gila project."

Clyde Kluckhohn and the Harvard Hornet's Nest

The intellectual landscape of Harvard in the prewar years had much to do with the content and direction of the Mogollon controversy. We think it may have conditioned the particular position that Brew took in publications and reviews and was reflected clearly in Walter W. Taylor's landmark critique of traditional archaeology, the 1943 Harvard dissertation published five years later as *A Study of Archaeology* (Taylor 1948). The architect of this intellectual landscape was the renowned cultural anthropologist Clyde Kay Mayben Kluckhohn, who in 1940 made his views crystal clear in a paper for a volume honoring Alfred Tozzer. In this work, titled "The Conceptual Structure in Middle American Studies," Kluckhohn extended his observations to include most of contemporary North American archaeology, and we think it appropriate that his words speak for themselves:

> To begin with, I should like to record an overwhelming impression that many students in this field [Middle American studies] are but slightly reformed antiquarians. To one who is a layman in these highly specialized realms there seems a great deal of obsessive wallowing in detail of and for itself. (Kluckhohn 1972:79)

No one, of course, has greater abhorrence of an archaeology which is on the intellectual level of stamp collecting than Dr. Kidder. In the Year Book of the Carnegie Institute he has insistently reaffirmed the necessity for "work of synthesis and exposition," for interpreting facts as well as collecting them. Little effort seems, however, to have been given to developing an explicit and consistent logical scheme for attaining these ends. Thus far the published record suggests that his staff are still predominately preoccupied with answering questions of a factual order. Dr. Kidder might reply that until we have a considerably fuller control of the facts generalization would be premature and misleading. Certainly the history of New World archaeology during this century gives us cause for alarm lest more synthetic interpretations which have an utterly inadequate observational basis become crystallized as sacrosanct dogmas. But warranted and stark synthesis is not to be identified in too cavalier a fashion with theory which means, first of all, examination of overt and covert premises (postulates and assumptions) and the general problem of the conceptualization of discrete data. There are, I think, grounds for believing that anthropologists generally have not quite kept on the forward march to the scientific frontiers in this respect. . . . In my observation the greater number of anthropologists still feel that "theorizing" is what you do when you are too lazy, or too impatient, or too much of an arm-chair person to go out and get the facts. (Kluckhohn 1972:81)

A system of theory in any science involves a small number of categories and elementary relations between them. . . . Ask any archaeologist to set forth and justify his conceptual scheme. It is an induction from my experience that the betting odds are enormous against this having even occurred to him as a problem. But if more archaeologists had given systematic thought to the logical implications of one concept which they continually use ("typology"), the problem of pottery classification in various areas in the New World would not be such a welter of confusion. Anthropologists generally have troubled themselves very little with what their conceptual tools actually meant if reduced to concrete human behaviors. (Kluckhohn 1972:82)

In these passages, Kluckhohn does not equivocate. He challenges archaeologists to rise above fact-grubbing antiquarianism to grapple with the epistemological and theoretical concepts and principles that should underlie their efforts to understand past human behavior. Kluckhohn's power and influence may have helped to set the agenda for the Harvard position in the Mogollon controversy.

As published in 1948, Taylor's 1943 dissertation was an expanded, full-length presentation of the Kluckhohn critique and a more complete expression of the troubled intellectual climate of American anthropological archaeology. Its representativeness of the intellectual climate may be surmised from the fact that Taylor's dissertation was accepted by the faculty in 1943, the same year that Reed's dissertation was rejected. Taylor's lengthy, ad hominem critique of Kidder may also have encouraged Kidder to shift his position on the Mogollon. In addition to the call for higher levels of conceptualization, Taylor's critique of almost every other prominent North and Middle American archaeologist of the day, including Haury, set a shrill tone for intellectual discourse during the 1940s.

Other archaeologists, however, were busy accumulating data to support Mogollon distinctiveness, antiquity, and validity. One of them, Paul Sidney Martin, was an intellectual power in his own right. In the following chapter, we return to the pivotal year 1939, when Haury began his field school in the Forestdale Valley. Our story takes us next to Pine Lawn Valley, New Mexico.

9
Pine Lawn Valley, New Mexico

> The Mogollon culture had been recently delineated as a
> separate branch by Haury, and his taxonomy and his theories
> were being combated. Hence I was eager to help substantiate
> his ideas, if possible. Also, little was known about the
> antecedents of the culture that Haury had unearthed.
>
> —Paul Sidney Martin (1974:13)

In 1939, when Haury began his field school in the Forestdale Valley, Paul Sidney Martin of the Chicago Field Museum of Natural History (Nash 2006) and his assistant, John B. Rinaldo, began a long-term program of site excavations run out of a field camp in the Pine Lawn Valley of west-central New Mexico (fig. 9.1). Today, the Martin and Rinaldo camp is gone, except for one lone, stone chimney and a scatter of broken glass and crockery, and the Pine Lawn locality itself is marked only by a roadside rest stop and the concrete remnants of what once was the store. Martin had selected this area for investigation from the survey records of the 1931 reconnaissance by Haury and Hastings, which showed a wealth of pit-house and pueblo sites throughout the San Francisco River drainage from Reserve to Glenwood. "Further, although I blush to admit it," wrote Martin (1974:13), "I was tired of the sage brush environment of Colorado and wanted to be in a pine forest—certainly the height of nonsense when one is supposed to be a scientist." Given our experience with the vicious Colorado Plateau gnat, the piranha of the insect world, we think Martin may have fled the sagebrush country because it hosted this invisible bloodsucker.

Gnats aside, there was much to recommend the Pine Lawn Valley. This stretch of mountain country, with its forests, meadows, and lush valleys, can appear ethereal when clad in summer's rich green, and the anvil shapes of thunderclouds spread miles high overhead. Glenwood, where they still remember Martin, drowses under huge, blooming trees filled

Figure 9.1 Paul Sidney Martin (left) and John Beach Rinaldo of the Field Museum of Natural History. (Courtesy of The Field Museum; neg. no. A93707)

with incessantly buzzing cicadas. It boasts the only motel within miles, the coldest Dos Equis Amber we have ever tasted, and the best breakfasts in the West. Few of these things were there more than a half-century ago, when the Chicago Field Museum of Natural History worked in the Pine Lawn Valley. It was the depth and extent of the archaeological record that drew Martin and his crew, and they were rewarded well.

Martin recalled (Martin and Rinaldo 1940) that Abajo Red-on-orange was the clue that lured him into the Mogollon controversy. He had found this unusual type in southwestern Colorado, and its origin was a mystery. At first, Martin believed it to be a Basketmaker invention, but gradually he was persuaded that the pottery was Mogollon in authorship or somehow related to Mogollon ceramics. Martin wanted to investigate its origin. The Pine Lawn region was ideal for this research, because its many archaeological sites were "uncontaminated" by an overlay of later "Puebloan" influence.

The work of Martin and Rinaldo and their later research with Elaine Bluhm was critical to the Mogollon controversy in two important respects: they excavated relentlessly, and they published site reports almost immediately through the anthropology series of the Chicago Field Museum of Natural History. Thus, Martin and colleagues amassed an immense, readily available record of evidence in support of the Mogollon concept that could not be dismissed by allegations of insufficient work. Notable "New Archaeologist" William A. Longacre (see chap. 13) had worked closely with Martin in Vernon, Arizona, and substantiated this evaluation of the Pine Lawn work: "When Paul began his work in the Mogollon area, the suggestion that the Mogollon Culture was a separate, even earlier development compared to the Anasazi was controversial to say the least. In no small part, the distinctiveness and priority of the Mogollon was demonstrated in the research that he directed" (1976:91).

The first contribution of the Chicago Field Museum expedition (Martin and Rinaldo 1940) appeared in 1940, the same year that Haury's Bear Village report was published. It was the first of three reports titled *The SU Site. Excavations at a Mogollon Village, Western New Mexico* (Martin 1943; Martin and Rinaldo 1947). The site was called the SU site after the brand of the old Stevenson-Underwood ranch (Martin 1974). Years ago, we were taught to pronounce it "Shoe"; this bit of lore has been lost to contemporary archaeologists, who pronounce the site name as two letters. In the admittedly preliminary 1940 report, Martin and Rinaldo estimated that the pit-house village was earlier than the Georgetown phase, the earliest Mogollon phase originally defined by Haury, and would date prior to AD 500. Subsequent excavations would confirm this initial estimate and define the Pine Lawn phase of the Mogollon.

One year after the first SU site report was published, Rinaldo (1941) attempted to settle the Mogollon problem once and for all in a well-reasoned paper. He laid out the elements of the controversy, listed

Mogollon traits, and proposed that these were sufficiently distinctive to accord Mogollon a separate taxonomic status. Rinaldo marshaled evidence to indicate an early date for Mogollon and acceded to the notion of Mogollon assimilation in the late period. This paper appears to have had no noticeable effect on the controversy, and we are at a loss to explain its lack of impact, other than to fall back to our "fog of war" excuse.

Evidence from the Pine Lawn field station continued to accumulate after Rinaldo's 1941 publication. Martin (1943) issued his second report on excavations at the SU site in which he tackled the analytic and comparative statements previously precluded by limited data. Most significant was Martin's definition of the Pine Lawn phase. Working back in time from Haury's tree-ring dates with cross-dated pottery, Martin placed the Pine Lawn phase earlier than AD 500. Much later, William Bullard (1962) would criticize this technique, but the reanalysis of tree-ring dates by the Laboratory of Tree-Ring Research some decades later (see chap. 13) supports Martin's interpretation.

The third and final SU site report, issued in 1947, confirmed the extension of the Mogollon cultural sequence back in time through the definition of the Pine Lawn phase in New Mexico. The Bluff Village report (Haury and Sayles 1947) confirmed Mogollon antiquity in Arizona based on tree-ring dating.

Around this time, Martin developed a psychosocial interpretation of Mogollon culture that would infuse his subsequent writings. Continuing to emphasize the earlier pit-house manifestations of Mogollon, Martin presented a tentative definition of Mogollon culture in which the significant points were its preceramic Cochise antecedents and post–AD 700 capitulation to overwhelming Anasazi influence. As he recalled many years later:

> I characterized the Mogollon culture as an undeveloped, unsophisticated, unalloyed, unvarnished, homespun kind of culture with no striking or dramatic features. The general pattern was unadorned and lowly and based on almost minimal requirements. It was homogeneous and non-expansive in that it probably sought no, or few contacts with other cultures. I conjectured that the people were mild, timid, and retiring. The traits that appeared in their region (houses, agriculture and pottery), were not reworked and were not stamped with strong Mogollon character or woven into the Mogollon pattern. I felt that the Mogollones never became accustomed to agriculture or

with house-building but continued to love and use their old house-hold "gods"—stone artifacts inherited from their Cochise ancestry. When Anasazi influences later drifted into their areas, the resistance of the Mogollon was so mild that the Anasazi culture became the dominant one. This was my evaluation of the Mogollon in 1943. (Martin 1974:14)

Martin maintained this interpretation throughout his long association with Mogollon research, although he would later modify it to permit him to label the post–AD 1000 pueblo-building people as Mogollon.

Books published in 1947—and there were several impressive archaeological works—were inconsistent in their perspectives on the Mogollon issue, despite the wealth of information issuing from New Mexico and Arizona. In their textbook, *Indians Before Columbus: Twenty Thousand Years of North American History Revealed by Archeology*, Martin, George Quimby, and John Collier (1947) fully endorsed the reality and importance of the Mogollon culture as Haury had defined it. In their chapter on "The Mogollon-Mimbres Culture," they provided the standard trait list for the New Mexico phase sequence of Pine Lawn, Georgetown, San Francisco, and Three Circle and concluded that the Mimbres phase was "more Anasazi than Mogollon."

By contrast, in her *Prehistoric Indians of the Southwest*, H. M. Wormington (1947) remained cautious under the guise of prudent objectivity. In a brief chapter on "The Mogollon Culture," she confessed that "writing about the Mogollon Culture is rather like dealing with a time bomb. It is impossible to ignore it, but one has the uncomfortable feeling that whatever one does about it is likely to be wrong." She went on to write (Wormington 1947:148): "In the relatively few years which have elapsed since it was first suggested that it was a separate entity and not just a regional variation of the Basketmaker-Pueblo pattern, there have come to be many theories. . . . Unfortunately, too few sites have been excavated to evaluate fully all the conflicting theories. It has been said that 'The Mogollon appears to be an illegitimate whose paternity is still under scrutiny.'"

Her comment that too few Mogollon sites had been excavated to evaluate all the conflicting theories surrounding the Mogollon concept underscores some of the inconsistencies of the Mogollon controversy. In support of this observation, Wormington (1947) listed ten Mogollon sites, including five Mimbres ruins, as compared with only six for the unquestioned

Hohokam, three of which—the Tonto Cliff Dwellings, Casa Grande National Monument, and Los Muertos—are sites of the Classic period with ambiguous Hohokam affiliations in Haury's (1945a) view.

Martin and Rinaldo continued to excavate and report rapidly on their work in the Pine Lawn Valley. They moved beyond demonstrating Mogollon separateness to grapple with problems at the early and late ends of the sequence. These important contributions included *Cochise and Mogollon Sites* (Martin, Rinaldo, and Antevs 1949), *Turkey Foot Ridge* (Martin and Rinaldo 1950b), and *Sites of the Reserve Phase* (Martin and Rinaldo 1950a). Martin and Rinaldo viewed Mogollon integrity as continuing until the Reserve phase, around AD 1000, when masonry architecture and Reserve Black-on-white pottery appeared to herald the arrival of Anasazi influences.

In 1952, Martin, Rinaldo, Bluhm, Hugh Cutler, and Roger Grange authored *Mogollon Cultural Continuity and Change: The Stratigraphic Analysis of Tularosa and Cordova Caves*, which, according to the standards of the times, conclusively validated the claims for Mogollon antiquity and continuity with the Cochise culture. At Tularosa Cave, where one of the longest Mogollon sequences was discovered, the authors extended the Pine Lawn phase back to 150 BC with radiocarbon dates and insinuated that the occupation might be as early as 500 BC (Martin 1974:21). The miracle of radiocarbon dating had become an indispensable technique for archaeologists working in areas or sites beyond the reach of tree-ring dating and a major element in any reconstruction about the past.

Perhaps never before in the course of Southwest archaeology had so few produced so many site reports so quickly after completing excavations. Martin and Rinaldo, aided by colleagues and assistants, amassed during the 1940s and 1950s an impressive array of information on the Mogollon. Those not swayed by argument or fact should have been convinced on the basis of sheer bulk alone. Bulk would play a critical role in the conclusion of the controversy, which happened about the time Martin and Rinaldo abandoned the Pine Lawn Valley to establish a field station in Vernon, Arizona.

Martin's summary of "the intentions that have motivated our work" in New Mexico, written in January 1957, provides a quick synopsis of American archaeology in the Southwest during the 1940s and early 1950s:

I should say at the outset that we picked the Reserve–Pine Lawn area as a field headquarters for long term investigation at the suggestion of two of our most valued friends and advisors, Dr. Emil W. Haury and Mr. E. B. Sayles, of the University of Arizona. In 1939, the region was archaeologically *terra incognita* and the Mogollon culture was then merely an infant, bawling lustily for attention, and marked by few with favor. Our aims have fluctuated somewhat from time to time, but essentially they are the same as those which stimulated our researches in Colorado (1929–38). These goals have been so well expressed by Steward (1955) that I can do no better than to paraphrase his comments:

Two main interests have been of primary concern to us and have provided our research goals. One of these was the search for and recognition of consistent interrelationships between cultural phenomena in order to establish similarities that might recur within or across cultural boundaries, or indeed even in historically separate areas. If such relationships and similarities could be established and if the particular lines of cultural evolution could be discovered, one might then be able to make systematized statements or formulations that would have possible predictive value. . . .

The other drive that guided us was an interest in the historical approach. The acquisition of historical data permits the description of a particular culture area in time and space in order to make it stand out in unique and bold relief. . . .

Obviously we have not completely fulfilled our ambitious ideals; but we hope that we may have provided documented, raw data that can later be synthesized by a Kidder or a Kroeber. (Martin 1959b:149–50)

In the summer of 1955, Rinaldo excavated Foote Canyon Pueblo in eastern Arizona (Rinaldo 1959), while Martin prepared for the following year's move to the new headquarters at Vernon, Arizona. The frenetic pace of excavation and publication would resume in the summer of 1957 (cf. Nash 2006).

Martin and Rinaldo were not alone in producing research that would support and refine the Mogollon culture concept. Throughout the 1940s, Erik K. Reed published papers on the Mogollon culture and the Mogollon controversy that by the end of the decade had expanded the original concept into a new cultural entity. We turn now to Reed, a story that takes us to northern New Mexico and its ancient capital city, Santa Fe.

10
The View from Santa Fe

> The most general current concept of the probable antiquity
> and importance of the Mogollon complex is accepted herein:
> and the term Mogollon will be used in its broader sense, not
> merely as referring only to sites excavated by Haury and
> Martin in southwestern New Mexico. Current usage of
> Mogollon to denote a major cultural "root" approximates
> Mera's "southern brownware complex," and applies to
> material all the way from the Pecos to the Verde.
>
> —Erik K. Reed (1942b:3)

In this chapter, we comment on the unsung hero of the Mogollon controversy and a remarkable archaeologist in his own right—Erik K. Reed.
Throughout the 1940s, Reed published papers on the Mogollon culture
and the Mogollon controversy, and by the end of the decade had expanded
the original concept into a new cultural entity that would resonate with
Mogollon archaeologists long after it was first proposed. Reed was a critical player in the Mogollon controversy. Several threads running through
this controversy come together in Reed's personal history and his part in
the Mogollon drama. We can see Harvard's strong influence in refusing
to recognize the Mogollon, the unspoken conflict pitting the academic
prestige of eastern universities against their upstart western counterparts,
and the critical importance of intellect in archaeological discovery, definition, and debate. We also glimpse the power of landscape in shaping
personality. One side of this drama was played out in Santa Fe, New
Mexico, where Reed settled and wrote his series of well-reasoned, thoughtful articles on the Mogollon.

Erik Kellerman Reed was born on August 16, 1914, in Quincy, Massachusetts, and grew up in Washington, D.C. His birth date is critical,
because the biographical sketch penned by Charlie Steen (1981)—a

longtime friend and colleague of Reed—failed to emphasize the incredible speed at which Reed raced through high school and university. According to Steen (1981:1–3): "He graduated from Washington Central High School and then entered George Washington University for his freshman year. Following that he spent three years at a ranch school at Deep Springs, California. . . . After the California years, he returned to G.W.U. and received a B.A. degree in the spring of 1932, with a major in anthropology."

In case the reader's math fails, in the spring of 1932, we note that Reed was only seventeen years old. Subtract three years in California and at least two years of college, and one arrives at an entering freshman age of around twelve years old. Deep Springs—an educational institution that survives today—also deserves a bit of commentary. Industrialist and pioneer electrical engineer L. L. Nunn founded the all-male, alternative school in 1917 on three principles: academics, labor, and self-governance. The school is a working ranch located in the Deep Springs Valley between the White and Inyo mountain ranges; the nearest sizable town is an hour away by car over a mountain pass. Deep Springs's physical isolation was designed to play a central role in the educational experience. Physical toil, book learning, and isolation would shape outstanding citizens, Nunn believed. High class standing was a prerequisite for admission to this extraordinary school, which provided full scholarships for twelve to twenty students.

Reed's attendance at Deep Springs is further testament to his personality. Deep Springs was a radical experiment, undertaken at a time when the United States was embroiled in war, intellectuals railed against American materialism, and Teddy Roosevelt's conservationist influence was still freshly felt in the West (*Christian Science Monitor*, February 19, 2002). Deep Springs also hints at the power of landscape in shaping Reed's personality. "The desert has a deep personality," wrote founder Nunn in 1923; "it has a voice. Great leaders in all ages have sought the desert and heard its voice. You can hear it if you listen, but you cannot hear it while in the midst of uproar and strife for material things" (Deep Springs College, http://www.deepsprings.edu/home [accessed May 23, 2009]).

We keep these facts in mind as we return to Steen's account:

To continue with Erik's academic career—he received an MA from Harvard in 1933 and passed the preliminary examinations for a PhD in 1934. For the summer of 1933 he was granted a Laboratory of Anthropology Fellowship and spent the season working with Frank H. H.

Roberts Jr. (of the Bureau of American Ethnology) at the Allantown Site, Arizona. His formal studies at Harvard were completed in the spring of 1934, and he spent that summer working under Emil W. Haury (then of Gila Pueblo, Globe, Arizona) at the Harris Site in the Mimbres area. (Steen 1981:1)

In the spring of 1934, when Reed completed all requirements except the dissertation at Harvard, he was nineteen; in the same spring, a somewhat older Haury defended his dissertation and received his Harvard PhD. Reed's precocious educational career and his obvious intellectual strength shine through.

Steen continued:

During the winter of 1934–35, [Reed] worked under Emil Haury on the great Snaketown excavation. After that came a succession of short jobs—appointment by the National Park Service as Seasonal Ranger at Hovenweep, Arches, and Yucca House National Monuments in the summer of 1935. Then in August 1935, there was a job with the State Parks Division of the Civilian Conservation Corps in which he supervised several archaeological projects, including the excavation of the Spanish Colonial Mission at Goliad, and during the summers of 1936 and 1937 made an archaeological survey of the area which was to become Big Bend National Park.

In March 1937, he was assigned administrative duties (for archaeology) at the National Park Service office at Santa Fe, New Mexico. This office became the Regional Office for NPS activities in the Southwest, and in 1939 Erik was appointed Regional Archaeologist. (Steen 1981:1–3)

In 1942, Reed carried on major excavations at sites in Mancos Canyon, Colorado. The work was conducted for the Bureau of Indian Affairs and the Ute Mountain Indian Agency because impending road construction threatened the sites. Steen observed that this project "was probably the first highway archaeological salvage project in this country" (1981:3). After volunteering for the army in 1943, Reed served in the European theatre of operations until March 1946. "While he was in the army, Harvard accepted his report on the Mancos Canyon excavations as a dissertation and Reed was granted the PhD degree" (1981:3). Reed returned to the National Park Service where he worked as regional archaeologist and regional chief of interpretation until his retirement in 1969. Reed lived in Santa Fe until his death.

Steen's account also did not mention that Reed's Harvard committee rejected *two* dissertations before his Mancos Canyon work was accepted as a dissertation in compensation. The second rejected dissertation was an expanded data presentation in support of arguments and interpretations he made in the first submission. In a September 26, 1943, letter to McGregor, Reed wrote, "Have been thus slow in replying to your good letter of Aug. 11 due to concentrating on finishing rewriting my thesis for resubmission before going into the Army. I'll finish it today easily, I think." In another letter to McGregor, dated March 3, 1947, Reed references "my thesis (the rejected one, not the Mancos Canyon report)." Reed made a similar reference to his rejected thesis in 1979 as a comment in the margin of an early manuscript that eventually grew into this book. Concerning a statement we had made about Kidder's early disbelief in Mogollon, Reed commented at the bottom of the page, "but Dr. Kidder liked my original thesis (the rejected one, not Mancos Canyon—well, it too)."

The first dissertation was titled "Cultural Continuities and Recombinations in the Southwest." Dated April 1942, it is 115 pages long, excluding references cited. The second dissertation, titled "Cultural Continuities in the Southwest" and dated September 1943, is 275 pages of text, footnotes, charts, and photographs. Although both may be considered to have been dissertation submissions, the latter document is "the rejected one" to which Reed referred in the above comment.

Despite its abbreviated length, there was much in the first, shorter dissertation that might have irritated Reed's Harvard advisors. In it, Reed set out to demonstrate the presence in central Arizona of "a group of important traits distinguishing that area from San Juan Anasazi and indicating a separate cultural subgroup here called the Western Pueblo complex" (Reed 1942b:3). Reed accepted without argument the distinctiveness and antiquity of the Mogollon and pointed out that the distribution of the culture embraced a much wider region than southwestern New Mexico, sweeping from "the Pecos to the Verde" (Reed 1942b:3). He observed the existence in the ancient Southwest of two broad cultural patterns labeled "Pueblo" and "Gila-Sonora." The former embraced two parallel but distinctive groups with temporal depth and regional character. The "early Puebloan group," characterized by pit-house architecture and flexed inhumation in common, consisted of "early Anasazi" and "Mogollon" subgroups that were distinguished by ceramics. The "late Puebloan group," characterized by masonry architecture and inhumation, comprised "developed Anasazi" and the new label, "Western Pueblo complex."

Reed went on to describe in detail the material-culture traits of the Western Pueblo and discuss sites by geographic region, supplementing the work with extensive citations. He also suggested some possible correlations between archaeology and ethnography. His conclusions include statements that may explain why this dissertation was met with disfavor:

> [I]t seems clear that a rich and important syncretistic cultural tradition which developed in the forested upland zone of central Arizona and expanded widely in late-prehistoric times to affect the entire Southwest is recognizable as distinct from the other—heretofore sometimes thought the only—major cultural division of the general Puebloan pattern, the Anasazi of the San Juan and upper Rio Grande. . . . [T]he various Western Pueblos, drawing on Anasazi and Hohokam sources as well as the Mogollon base, developed a complex and advanced cultural pattern which seemingly contributed major elements to the historic Pueblo groups. (Reed 1943:274–75)

A detailed set of appendices considered burial methods in the San Juan area, orange ware in the San Juan area, the three-quarter-grooved axe, black-on-white pottery in the Little Colorado and Gila River drainages, language, and physical type. In the appendix focusing on San Juan Orange Ware, Reed also set forth some notions that surely irritated his Mogollon-phobic committee. Abajo Red-on-orange, a type never satisfactorily explained, and other orange wares represented "a continuous development of oxidized painted pottery. . . . Evidently originating (presumably through Mogollon inspiration) in southeastern Utah," this tradition was indigenous throughout the western Anasazi region (1942b:88).

These notions were developed further in the second, longer rejected dissertation. It is alleged to have been too theoretical for Reed's committee, and indeed the dissertation is a synthesis of Southwest prehistory that could have easily been transformed into a textbook summary, much like what McGregor had done in 1941. In addition to the obvious synthetic quality, it was also aggressively supportive of the Mogollon concept. In the chapter titled "Complexes of Mogollon Derivation," Reed listed Mimbres, Chihuahua, the Dragoon complex of southeastern Arizona, the El Paso region, Mesilla, Peñasco Bend, and Alamogordo in addition to the better-known Forestdale Valley and southwestern New Mexico. By implication, such widespread geographic distribution belied the common Mogollon characterization as "backwater" Anasazi. Reed spent a paragraph on the Mogollon concept, noting that it was accepted by virtually all southwestern archaeologists, although rather tentatively by some. Colton (1939) and Haury (1940) had effectively answered Nesbitt's objections, the most recent critique at the time of Reed's writing.

Reed went further than Haury, Martin, or Rinaldo in extending Mogollon culture well beyond the estimated AD 700–1000 period of Anasazi assimilation and loss of identity. Other than masonry architecture and black-on-white pottery, Reed (1943:23) alleged "few distinctively Anasazi traits enter the Mogollon area and Mogollon cultures; I see no submergence and 'blotting out' of Mogollon by a 'tremendous amount' of 'virile' Anasazi influence to produce a hybrid 'blend.'" The late cultural developments differed from early Mogollon through the addition of surface pueblos "in exactly the same ways that late Anasazi developments differ from Basket Maker" (Reed 1943:23). In addition to extending the Mogollon into pueblo-building times, Reed derived them from the preceramic Cochise culture, thus offering a vigorous and distinctive Mogollon culture throughout the prehistoric ceramic period.

What may have been the most galling claim to Reed's committee members in this rather breathtaking synthesis was that the Mogollon concept was vital to a thorough understanding of the prehistory of the Southwest. In its guise as Western Pueblo, the Mogollon swept into the Salado region of southern Arizona—"The Salado branch is essentially a division of the Cibola branch" (Reed 1943:177)—and on to Zuni, Acoma, and Hopi, and into the valley of the Rio Grande.

The irony in Harvard's rejecting Reed's dissertation as "too theoretical," one that has gone unexplained by students of southwestern archaeology, is that Walter W. Taylor's dissertation was accepted by the Harvard faculty in 1943, and it was exclusively a theoretical treatment of American archaeology that far exceeded Reed's cultural-historical synthesis. It seems to us highly likely that it was Reed's choice of subject matter and his interpretations that were unacceptable, not the theoretical nature of the dissertation. All was not lost, however. Reed's rejected dissertation would serve as the foundation for his papers on the Mogollon that appeared throughout the 1940s.

Reed's notions of Mogollon and Western Pueblo had clearly been forming before he wrote either of his rejected dissertations. In a three-page article on American archaeology written for the *National Park Service, Region III Quarterly* (1941), Reed foreshadowed the Western Pueblo concept by observing that certain National Park Service archaeological monuments were "not strictly Anasazi, probably being connected ultimately with a distinct cultural root known as 'Mogollon,' but they are of a general Pueblo type." Later, his 1943 manuscript on Mancos Canyon would suggest calling Anasazi and Mogollon by the single term "Pueblo." Brew (1946) happily underscored this notion in his Alkali Ridge report, because it confirmed for him that even Mogollon supporters could not distinguish Mogollon and Anasazi—although that clearly was not Reed's interpretation.

In a short paper titled "Implications of the Mogollon Concept," Reed (1942a) challenged the conservative position in terse and telling terms. He noted a definitional problem—one of merging a broad concept of Mogollon with the original complex defined by Haury. He agreed with Brew that the question of Mogollon separateness was one of taxonomy, but added that the question could not be discussed, much less resolved, until all participants settled on a single definition for a culture. The importance of the Mogollon concept was that it demanded reorientation of basic notions and approaches in southwestern archaeology. "It completes the breakup of traditionalist thought, the conception of the single center with its peripheries being replaced by several cultural areas or lineages with their separate sequences and interrelated history" (Reed 1942a:31). As an aside, it is one of those little ironies of history that in the early 1940s, Haury—later excoriated as an archtraditionalist—was credited with a scheme that "completes the breakup of traditionalist thought."

In 1944, Reed addended his previous views by beginning to take issue with points gaining currency among the pro-Mogollon faction. His review of Martin's (1943) second season at the SU site prompted the observation that Mogollon should be applied to "material of a general type from the Pecos to the Verde" (Reed 1944). He drew further attention to a logical oddity in stating that the term *Mogollon* should not be defined only in terms of its earliest known phases, because none defined Hohokam or Anasazi by their earliest phases. Combining this point with his dissatisfaction with Martin's description of the Mogollon as mild, timid, retiring, nonexpansive, conservative folk, Reed maintained that the Mogollon did not disappear under a wave of Anasazi influence in the second millennium AD. From those who would see the Mogollon being "swamped," "I should like to see a list of the specific traits known (not merely assumed) to be of Anasazi origin which constitute the surge of overwhelming Anasazi influence which supposedly poured into the Mimbres–White Mountains area to dominate and submerge the Mogollon culture" (Reed 1944:362). He requested another list of those cultures that remained pure.

These lists seem not to have been provided, and for this reason, perhaps, Reed (1946) was prompted to offer lists of his own—one for Anasazi and the other for Mogollon—to support further his view of Mogollon distinctiveness, antiquity, and continuity into the post–AD 1000 period. In this paper, Reed published the Western Pueblo concept outlined in his dissertations; he would express the notion in print more fully in subsequent articles. This paper marked the appearance of another conception of Mogollon, one emphasizing cultural continuity between the pit-house and pueblo builders.

Perhaps Reed was a trifle too optimistic when in 1946 he wrote that "the separateness and antiquity of Mogollon are now generally admitted" (1946:297). One would certainly have thought this to be the case, with its geographical spread and material continuity established by the Mogollon, Harris, Bluff, Bear, and SU sites and tree-ring dates extending back to AD 300. The relationship of the preceramic Cochise culture to the Mogollon had been securely argued to account for cultural change at the beginning of the sequence. It seemed the most pressing problem was to interpret Anasazi influence and Mogollon identity at the late, pueblo-building end of the sequence. Reed's optimism oversimplified the situation. As we have seen in previous chapters, heated discussion over the fundamental issues continued with renewed vigor as tradition, authority, and power struggled to prevail.

In 1950, having long argued for the distinctiveness of Mogollon, Reed completed the publication of his summary of traits that set Mogollon apart from the Anasazi. Associated with the Anasazi were circular kivas, black-on-white and gray-ware pottery, full-grooved axes, flexed inhumation, and lambdoidal cranial deformation resulting from infant cradleboarding. By contrast, the Mogollon possessed square kivas; polished, brown plain ware, red-slipped pottery, and a variety of painted types; three-quarter-grooved axes; extended inhumation; and vertical-occipital cranial deformation resulting from use of a different kind of cradleboard. Reed concluded that the Mogollon probably received black-on-white pottery and masonry from the Anasazi, but in a later paper, Reed (1956) pointed out that the pueblo layout plan was quite different between the two—the Anasazi employed a unidirectional plan and the Mogollon a layout inwardly focused on one or more plazas.

Although there were similarities between the Anasazi and Mogollon after AD 1000 that constituted a general pueblo pattern in contrast to the Hohokam, the differences required recognition through the use of separate cultural labels. Mindful of the general similarities and specific differences, Reed had suggested the term *Western Pueblo* for the Mogollon of this period. Reed never seemed unduly bothered by what label should be employed, however, and perhaps for this reason, later investigators felt free to misapply his terms.

Reed asserted that there was no basis for viewing the Anasazi as having swamped or assimilated the post–AD 1000 Mogollon because the traits he contrasted continued throughout the pueblo-building period. He stressed that far from being peripheral, the Western Pueblo development was "a complex and advanced cultural pattern and seemingly contributed major elements to the historic Western Pueblos and to a lesser degree also to the upper Rio Grande" (Reed 1950:136). In point of fact, Reed even insinuated that the Mogollon may have assimilated the Anasazi in the centuries after AD 1300.

Reed never published his rejected second dissertation as a textbook synthesis of southwestern prehistory rivaling Kidder's or McGregor's works. It is clear, however, that by focusing on the essential elements of Mogollon–Western Pueblo continuity and peppering the southwestern literature with his papers, Reed contributed an astonishing clarity of vision and an abundance of well-researched information to supporting and refining the Mogollon concept. It would be Haury who would take the argument to the next level—defending the Mogollon in the dirt of Point of Pines, Arizona.

11
Point of Pines, Arizona

> Apart from its unsurpassed archaeological riches, [Point of
> Pines was] imbued with a particular and hard to describe
> mystique, the vista across Circle Prairie to the White
> Mountains uncluttered by twentieth century scars; its
> isolation where train whistles were unknown and where
> the overhead noise of airplanes was seldom heard; where the
> surrounding topography made access easy to most of the
> places the archaeologist wanted to visit; where by mid-August
> the rains brought out an eye-dazzling display of wild flowers;
> where the air of the day and the night was soft and clear,
> untouched with other than atmospheric haze; and where at
> summer's end one did not want to leave to face the stress of
> urban existence.
>
> —Emil Haury, quoted in Gifford and Morris (1985:402)

The year 1946 was a pivotal one for the Mogollon controversy. The pro-Mogollonist and the anti-Mogollonist factions had established their positions, and the former had been busily compiling new data in support of their arguments. Haury had been at the University of Arizona for almost a decade. The war had ended, freeing personnel and funds for archaeological research once more. The time had come, Haury believed, to rebuild and lay plans for the future. In 1946, Haury moved the University of Arizona Archaeological Field School to Point of Pines on the San Carlos Apache Reservation, surely one of the most remote and stunning places in Arizona (fig. 11.1).

The archaeology of this extraordinary place would play the crucial role in resolving the Mogollon controversy, and in this chapter, we give Point of Pines the importance it deserves. We present evidence to support our contention that the strategic orchestration of the Point of Pines

Figure 11.1 The University of Arizona Archaeological Field School camp at Point of Pines on the San Carlos Apache Reservation, with Circle Prairie in the background. (Courtesy of the Arizona State Museum)

archaeological record and graduate-student research brought a convincing conclusion to the Mogollon controversy. The Pecos Conferences of 1948 and 1951 were held there to showcase Mogollon pit houses in situ. Most important, it was no accident that the synthetic work that would resolve the Mogollon controversy was born at Point of Pines. This was Joe Ben Wheat's (1955) *Mogollon Culture Prior to A.D. 1000.*

Point of Pines is located in the mountain Transition Zone of Arizona, the most highly dissected, precipitous region in the state. It also is one of the best-watered locales in the mountains, representing what we have called an "island of resource advantage" for its proximity to land, water, and other resources in a vast region where these advantages are scarce. Point of Pines is north of the basalt plateau called Nantack Ridge that divides the Gila and Salt river drainages. Eagle Creek and Willow Creek drain the area, and to the north is the Black River.

By this time in his career, Haury had worked at Forestdale Valley and had surveyed most of east-central Arizona while with Gila Pueblo. He knew its forests and meadows were thick with masonry-pueblo ruins. Why, then, did he choose the Point of Pines locale as the scene for playing out the Mogollon drama? Haury's recollections provide a variety of motives from which to choose.

In 1945, a quick trip to Point of Pines had suggested the area to be a prime target for research, but its suitability for a long-term field-training camp had to be proved. With a grant from the Wenner-Gren Foundation for Anthropological Research, Haury and Sayles spent six weeks surveying the region from Pole Corral to Eagle Creek on the San Carlos Apache Reservation, roughly seven hundred square miles (Haury 1989). They discovered some two hundred sites, spanning the entire range of pit houses to small, surface pueblos to huge pueblos containing hundreds of rooms. In addition, they found small cliff ruins and historical Western Apache camps. In his personal reminiscence—*Point of Pines, Arizona: A History of the University of Arizona Field School*—Haury (1989) stressed the richness of the archaeological remains as a foundation for long-term field training of students. Point of Pines surely would meet the needs of the field school that was planned to be in operation for twelve to fifteen years.

Haury knew, of course, that Point of Pines lay in the heartland of the Mogollon country. He wrote (Haury 1989:9), "[T]he region was inhabited in early times by people who could be linked with the Mogollon culture, whose traces had been studied rather thoroughly in Mogollon Village and in the Forestdale Valley." In this way, "The training of students in a variety of archaeological techniques and interpretative problems could go hand-in-hand with contributing to the knowledge of a little-known region, thereby adding a freshness and seriousness of purpose to the venture" (Haury 1989:9). This statement seemingly underplayed the significance of the archaeological record to the Mogollon controversy.

A slightly different ordering of selection priorities derives from Haury's foreword to Fred Wendorf's *A Report on the Excavation of a Small Ruin Near Point of Pines, East Central Arizona*:

In short, this seemed to be the spot where a correlation of the histories of the Pueblo, Hohokam, and Mogollon could be made, if this were possible anywhere. Furthermore, the availability of woods for buildings forecasts the possibility of recovering such materials which would aid in establishing a chronology in terms of the Christian calendar by tree-ring dating. . . . Aside from the research aspects, the University of Arizona also had a desire to establish an archaeological field school, keeping alive a tradition of long standing and providing the opportunity for practical field experience to ambitious students of archaeology. (Haury 1950b:7–8)

Haury's personal reminiscences allude to what we believe was the true motivation for taking the field school to Point of Pines. Not the least of the area's attractions, Haury said:

> was the fact that the early villages of the area all exhibited heavy concentrations of brownware of the kinds we had seen in the Forestdale Valley and in the western edges of New Mexico. That ceramic complex was clearly the hallmark of the Mogollon people. Point of Pines, therefore, promised to yield much new information on a problem that had previously occupied my mind. All manner of problems and challenges could be envisioned. The resources were there to fuel many years of work. (Haury 1979:155–56)

We conclude that Haury had definite research motives in addition to pedagogy that led him to move the field school to Point of Pines.

Having made the decision, the first order of business was to construct a comfortable camp in the beautiful but isolated location. Today, one can go to Point of Pines easily from the Apache Gold Resort and Casino over paved roads most of the way in about an hour. This was scarcely the case in 1946. Haury (1989) related the tortuous seventy-five-mile journey from San Carlos to Point of Pines at great length in an effort to convey to the modern reader the field camp's isolation and the ruggedness of the surrounding country. The spot Haury selected for his camp was a magical locale. On a low ridge of firm ground, it lay in a fringe of pines threading into the magnificent vastness of Circle Prairie. As Wendorf (1950:15) wrote, "A view of the area from the Nantack Ridge would show a vast prairie 20 or more miles in length and 10 miles in width, interrupted at intervals by clumps of juniper, oak, and occasionally pine." Around the campsite in all directions were the ruins the archaeologists had come to investigate, and the White Mountains provided the backdrop to it all.

The "camp" Haury constructed was a paragon of comfort and built to last—a cluster of frame buildings including a dining room–kitchen complete with picture window and fireplace, laboratory, bath house, infirmary, staff quarters, and student cabins. A power plant provided electricity, and a huge walk-in cooler served to keep trips to Globe, the nearest town with services, as few as possible. The manager of the Phelps-Dodge pumping plant on the Black River witched a well that poured cold and sweet water at precisely the depth the manager had predicted. Whether it was achieved by luck, common sense, or good planning, everything conspired to create a field school that made history.

Most of Haury's (1989) history of this special place and time is devoted to camp logistics, lists of accomplishments, personal reminiscences, and a smattering of retrospective rationalization. When he wrote that history, the Mogollon controversy had been finalized in Haury's mind for thirty years or more, and the part Point of Pines played in its demise was either a minor memory or another instance of Mennonite-bred modesty. We think the latter.

That first summer, Haury chose a team of ten men, mostly veterans, to build the camp and begin exploring the archaeology of Point of Pines. It did not take long for both camp and archaeology to expand, not only training a great number of professional archaeologists but providing the ultimate solution to the Mogollon problem.

The 1946–1948 Seasons

Ground was broken on June 2, 1946, on the first site at Point of Pines, a small, twenty-one-room masonry pueblo next to the large Point of Pines Ruin, numbered AZ W:10:51 in the Arizona State Museum system. Wendorf's (1950) report provides little in the way of a research rationale for tackling this particular site, although Haury made it clear in his history of Point of Pines that practicality drove its selection: the men could excavate while at the same time building the camp. The excavations were completed the next season. Haury (1989:17) noted that the ruin presented two surprises. A great number of well-preserved, domestic artifacts lay as they were abandoned on the room floors, and pit structures dating to Pueblo III times lay below the masonry rooms, suggesting the contemporaneity of pit structures and aboveground pueblos in the region. Haury also stressed the importance of tree-ring dating to the Point of Pines research program.

Wendorf (1950) defined two late phases in Point of Pines prehistory on the basis of excavations at AZ W:10:51, but he contributed little to the Mogollon concept beyond suggesting that the introduction of masonry-pueblo architecture was not accomplished via large-scale immigration "but by the gradual adaptation on the part of the pit house people or their cultural descendants" (1950:146). As one might expect, given his lifelong refusal to concede that the mountain inhabitants after AD 1000 could be Mogollon, Haury (1989) referred to the pueblo-builders as Anasazi throughout his reminiscences.

In 1947, work began on the big ruin, AZ W:10:50. An exciting discovery was the presence of an enormous great kiva with rock-covered trenches in the floor and a huge, central hearth. In 1948, the great kiva was excavated, depressions thought to be reservoirs or possible kivas were investigated, and a few pit houses at Crooked Ridge Village some three miles from camp were excavated. Haury (1989:45) recalled that the pit structures were investigated "not only to bring us face-to-face with the Mogollon problem, but to provide show pieces, along with our work in pueblo structures, for the Pecos conferees expected to gather at our camp late in August." Haury wanted the conference attendees "to see what an early Mogollon village had to offer and in what respects it differed from roughly contemporary Anasazi villages farther north" (Haury 1989:50).

The 1948 Pecos Conference and a Model of Academic Discourse

The Pecos Conference is a long and hallowed tradition in the anthropology of the American Southwest. Richard Woodbury (1993) has chronicled the history of the Pecos Conference through 1988, and we draw heavily upon his research and insights. The eleventh Pecos Conference and the first held outside of New Mexico took place at the Point of Pines field-school camp on August 24, 25, and 26, 1948. To shelter the guests, Haury set up twenty-three tents in addition to the permanent buildings. The kitchen crew served three meals in three sittings every day, surely straining a kitchen crew unaccustomed to feeding more than 130 people. The theme of the conference, Haury (1989:51) wrote, was "the Mogollon culture and the transition to Anasazi in late times." The conference brought together many of the major antagonists in the Mogollon controversy— Martin, Brew, Reed, Rinaldo, Kidder, and of course, Haury.

Through the stenographic skill of Pat Wheat, Joe Ben Wheat's wife, we have a transcription of the Mogollon session that documents the conceptual position of the principal participants and the informality of the exchange. The record shows that Martin avidly supported a distinct Mogollon culture, in contrast to Brew's objection to its status as a separate culture on the basis of too few distinctive traits. Haury, host of the conference, was resolute and concise, permitting others to voice strong opinions. Reed displayed the same patience and consistent presentation of facts that marked his position throughout the 1940s. This dialogue in the pines was a defining moment in the Mogollon controversy.

According to Woodbury:

> The most important event of the Conference took place the next morning [August 26]—a panel discussion on the Mogollon culture cochaired by Sayles and Martin. As Haury (1949a) reported in *American Antiquity*, "This discussion, lively and informative at times, obtuse at other times, did at least bring certain problems into the open and showed the great need for more energetic wielding of the shovel." There is an oral tradition, which has been confirmed by Haury (letter to Woodbury, 19 May 1986), that when the panel was seated Brew's place was marked by a basketball on which a large white "8" had been painted, reflecting his minority position, on the defensive as the skeptic who doubted the utility or justification of the Mogollon concept. (Woodbury 1993:178)

Other panelists were Haury, Reed, Kidder—who had been an honored guest at the camp in the previous summer—Harold S. Colton (Museum of Northern Arizona), Sayles, Donald Lehmer (a University of Chicago graduate student who was on the Point of Pines staff that summer), Rinaldo (Martin's field director at Pine Lawn), and Stanley Stubbs (Laboratory of Anthropology). The knowledge and experience of this group are impressive. According to Woodbury (1993:178–81), "Martin began by reading from an article by Brew and Edward B. Danson (a University of Arizona student who was doing his graduate work with Brew at Harvard University), which said, in part: 'Between the two [Anasazi and Hohokam] an enigmatic Mogollon culture is postulated, an intriguing prospect as yet not supported by a sufficient number of distinct traits to give it validity as a useful concept in our historical reconstructions' (Brew and Danson 1948:211–22)."

"Having thus thrown down Brew's gauntlet, so to speak," Woodbury continued, "Martin yielded the floor to Brew, who elaborated his doubts about and objections to the Mogollon concept. As recorded by Pat Wheat, Brew said:

> To explain the situation, we have the Pueblo people—not a linguistic classification, but we have a culture; Hohokam sites dug by Gila Pueblo produced a number of striking traits. It seemed reasonable to think

that the archaeologists had discovered something for which there was enough evidence to substantiate defining a separate culture. We are in a stage in our own culture where the cautious person winds up behind the 8-ball. Herbie Dick, on the Peabody Museum Expedition has been incorporated as the early man division of the Upper Gila Expedition. The association he has there of a considerable amount of perishable material with Alma Plain pottery gives us a lot more to work with and to compare in order to see if this manifestation down here actually is of the nature which people as a whole call "culture." The difference between myself and the people here is that they may be using an archaeological definition which seems to be a confusing rather than a useful technique. (P. Wheat 1948:30)

(We interrupt at this point to provide an editorial note. The transcribed record of Brew's views may be taken as an accurate representation of his comments, because he had the opportunity to review and revise Pat Wheat's original manuscript. Brew requested a copy of the transcript, but, because none existed, Haury sent him the original. Martin's quote from Brew and Danson, for example, exists as a handwritten, interlinear addition by Brew to the Wheat manuscript. He amended or added to his transcribed remarks at other points in the manuscript.)

Now, returning to Woodbury's chronicle, Martin responded, in part (again quoting Pat Wheat's record): "There is in my estimation, a fallacy in Brew's approach. E. W. Haury is the father of the Mogollon, published first on it, and has some pertinent remarks to make." Haury then said:

I am not the first man who had the idea. [Harry P.] Mera recognized some separation ceramically from the northern materials. We came into this material through a survey for Gila Pueblo from Reserve, New Mexico, down into the Mimbres. During the course of a large survey you pick up differences in cultures of people. As a direct result of these original surveys we excavated the Harris site and Mogollon Village in New Mexico. Will take the blame for the name. Felt it would be better to bring something out rather than to leave it unpublished. . . . I can see the Mogollon as an entity occupying a large geographical area, as large as the Basketmakers and larger than the Hohokam. (P. Wheat 1948:31)

There followed spirited exchanges concerning the nature of archaeological cultures, the distinguishing features of those cultures, Mogollon influences on other cultures, and the character of the Mogollon culture after AD 1000. Quotations from the Wheat manuscript presented in the appendix will provide a sense of the conversation that took place that August morning in 1948 and give the flavor of civilized discourse that characterized the debate. Woodbury (1993:183) concluded his summary of the conference with the comment that "There have been other Pecos Conference symposia on contested issues, but probably none more important in defining the issues of a major controversy."

In contrast to Woodbury's account, Haury (1989:51) recollected that "Although diverse subjects were discussed and there were the usual up-to-the-minute reports of work in progress, the main theme of the conference was the Mogollon culture and the transition to Anasazi in late times . . . . Since Pat Wheat (Mrs. Joe Ben Wheat), a skilled stenographer, kept a detailed record of the meeting, no more need be said about the conference here." We believe that Haury had planned well in advance of the conference an "argument with the shovel" more convincing to archaeologists of that era than an argument of words.

In the Point of Pines history, Haury (1989:50) recalled a bit of information that reveals the crucial role Crooked Ridge Village would play as well as his own faith in the ability of fieldwork to resolve issues and in the importance of data. "Toward the end of the season," he wrote, "we readied several pit houses at Crooked Ridge Village as a demonstration for the upcoming Pecos Conference. . . . Luckily, Joe Ben Wheat, who was in charge, had encountered a burned house that was especially productive of the kinds of residue one does not ordinarily find. Besides architectural charcoal, there were carbonized corn and beans and what appeared to be a fragment of charred sandal. These were good omens for the productivity of the site, and we concentrated on it in the following years" (Haury 1989:50). And concentrate on it they did. Crooked Ridge Village would be the centerpiece of Joe Ben Wheat's dissertation and contribute to resolution of the controversy.

Haury (1989:52) concluded his discussion of the 1948 field season with characteristic brevity and cautious optimism: "In retrospect, 1948 had been a good year, the best part being that we were getting our teeth into real archaeological problems, and the shape of what had to be done in future years was taking form. It was clear that advances would be slow and that progress in knowledge would come in small increments." Crooked Ridge Village would prove to be a much larger and significant data increment, and we turn to this pit-house village next.

12
Crooked Ridge Village

> Finally, the excavation of Crooked Ridge Village has led to
> the establishment of another regional variant, the Black
> River Branch, of the Mogollon Culture Pattern.
>
> —Joe Ben Wheat (1954a:182)

Perhaps by the end of the 1948 season, the strategic plan for resolving the Mogollon controversy was taking firmer shape in Haury's mind. The scatter of brown plain ware and red ware on the surface of Crooked Ridge Village indicated an early village of substantial size, and several pit houses had been excavated late in the 1948 season. Haury's next move was to put Wheat in charge of the Crooked Ridge Village excavations during the 1949 field season. Haury recalled:

> The time had come to assign specific research goals to students who were advanced enough in their training to manage work crews of Apaches and who would be able to follow a course eventually leading to the write-up and publication of results. The first to be accorded this independence was Joe Ben Wheat, and the ruin for which he was responsible was Crooked Ridge Village (AZ W:10:15), an early Mogollon site. . . . Wheat spent several seasons on this site; it provided the material for his doctoral dissertation and his work was published (Wheat 1954a, 1955). Most importantly, the work on Crooked Ridge Village represented the solid beginning of the Point of Pines chronology and clear evidence that the initial pottery-making and agricultural people of the region were those of the Mogollon culture. (Haury 1989:53)

The Mogollon of Crooked Ridge Village

Crooked Ridge Village is located on a long, narrow, branching ridge about three miles from Point of Pines. When Wheat dug there and probably also in prehistory, the ridge was a grassy, low slope dotted with pines over-looking a valley cut by an intermittent stream—a locale that was ideally suited for floodwater farming. Four seasons of fieldwork there would excavate 24 pit structures among an estimated 100 and define a new regional variant of the Mogollon culture, the Black River Branch (Wheat 1954a:7).

Domestic architecture included three different house types—rectangular (nearly square) or bean-shaped houses with simple ramped entryways; rectangular or round houses with vestibule entryways; and rectangular houses with southern annexes. Like other Mogollon houses, most of the Crooked Ridge pit structures were true pit houses with long, covered entries and four-post roof-support systems. Ceremonial structures were large and round with combined ramp-and-ladder or stepped entries, unusual floor features (floor drums?), and possible pilasters in the walls.

Pottery was limited to Alma Plain, Point of Pines and Black River varieties (distinguished by the nature of inclusions); variants of Alma Plain, such as Alma Rough and Alma Smudged; and San Francisco Red. Nonlocal pottery from other Mogollon regions, Hohokam ceramics, Anasazi ceramics, and a locally made version of Dos Cabezas Red-on-brown also were found. Types such as Mogollon Red-on-brown, Vahki Plain, Sweetwater Red-on-buff, and Snaketown Red-on-buff were considered consistent with the Circle Prairie phase occupation of Crooked Ridge; the presence of Kiatuthlanna Black-on-white and Gila Butte Red-on-buff suggested a later occupation following the Circle Prairie occupation, and a handful of Santa Cruz Red-on-buff sherds seemed inconsistent with other cross-dated ceramics. Unfortunately, tree-ring samples did not yield dates, and the site was dated solely by ceramic means.

The early Circle Prairie phase at Crooked Ridge equated with the Georgetown phase of the Mimbres Branch, the Dos Cabezas phase of the San Simon region, and the Hilltop phase of the Forestdale Valley. The late Circle Prairie phase was equivalent to the postulated San Lorenzo, Pinaleño, and Cottonwood phases of these regions, respectively.

In placing Crooked Ridge Village in its cultural context, Wheat (1954a:181) left no doubt about his views. "The architecture is basically Mogollon," he wrote, "although it varies from the eastern Mogollon." Ceramically, "Crooked Ridge Village is clearly Mogollon. The types of pottery—Alma Plain, Alma Rough, Alma Smudged, Alma Textured, and San Francisco Red—are part and parcel of the Mogollon tradition." To that, Wheat added the broad-line red-on-brown pottery. And finally, "All categories of artifacts [other than pottery] belong to the Mogollon patterns and extend them." Combining these typical Mogollon traits with the minor variations Wheat observed in architecture, vessel forms, the quantity of sand-tempered pottery, and so on, Wheat concluded that he had defined a new variant of the Mogollon, the Black River Branch.

But before Wheat's conclusions were published, Haury would bring the 1951 Pecos Conference back to Point of Pines, and Crooked Ridge Village would again serve as the evidentiary star in the fieldwork demonstration of Mogollon validity.

The 1951 Pecos Conference at Point of Pines

The summer of 1951 was uncharacteristically dry. The Independence Day celebration was canceled, and students were recruited to fight the fires that broke out across the reservation. Under those circumstances, it is difficult to imagine Haury taking on another Pecos Conference at the end of a directorial field-school season only three years after he had hosted one, unless he had a compelling reason for doing so. We think that reason was further validation of Mogollon in the field and in open discussion. Haury would never again host a Pecos Conference at Point of Pines.

Woodbury (1993:206–10) wrote that it was Haury who "suggested a session on 'the north versus the south pueblos problem' . . . in the light of Erik Reed's ideas in the S.J.A. [*Southwestern Journal of Anthropology*]" (Reed 1946, 1950)." The last day of the conference, Friday, August 17, 1951, began with the second roundtable, which was titled "Northern and Southern (or Eastern and Western) Pueblos," which Reed chaired. According to Woodbury:

> [Reed] summarized the evidence for a significant cultural distinction between the "northern" area (circular kivas, black-on-white or gray pottery, lambdoidal cranial deformation, full-grooved stone axes, and domestication of the turkey) and the "southern" area (rectangular kivas, brown pottery, occipital deformation, and the three-quarter grooved axe). These ideas were what Haury had in mind in his suggestion to Withers, and they had been published by Reed in the articles mentioned above, as well as in articles in *El Palacio* in 1948 and 1949. Thus the speakers in this roundtable were already familiar with Reed's position, and they tended to discuss local variations and

exceptions, or additional distinctions of possible importance. (Woodbury 1993:206–10)

Haury's own account of this event is excruciatingly terse and sheds no light on the Mogollon controversy:

> In 1951, we were the host institution once again to the Pecos Conference. A skeleton crew of students was carried over to help with preparations, putting up tents, peeling potatoes, and the like. The register showed 112 names and a fee of $10 was levied to help defray expenses, one of the first times this was done, because the camp budget would not stand the extra expenses. In all, 1,014 meals were served. Apart from introducing attendees to the work we were doing, there were the usual reports by others and several general sessions. As a special attraction, we engaged a troop of Devil Dancers [mountain spirit, or *ga'an,* dancers] from San Carlos who put on a performance Thursday evening, August 16, the first time that many conferees had seen these impressive masked dancers. (Haury 1989:65)

Haury may have been unconsciously predicting the future in his choice of words. The Harvard crew would soon begin bedeviling him anew.

The Harvard Counterattack

The conferences at Point of Pines and the impressive physical demonstration of Mogollon distinctiveness in the field seem not to have made an impression on the anti-Mogollon faction, for the Peabody Museum shortly began to prepare a counterattack. Previously, we called attention to the fact that Brew and Donald Scott had planned an expedition to New Mexico during the 1930s to explore the upper Gila River drainage, an area intermediate between the Anasazi and Mogollon homelands. The project was designed ostensibly to test the Mogollon culture concept. The Upper Gila Expedition was begun in 1947 near Quemado, New Mexico. The Harvard *Crimson* noted the beginning of this expedition on April 28, 1949. According to the article, Brew believed the Southwest was an "extremely fertile" field for archaeologists because it was so remote as to be essentially "untouched by previous expeditions." Even at that time, Brew was convinced of the area's cultural affiliation: the region "contains remains of civilizations which were predecessors of the Pueblos."

This research project not only shows Brew's commitment to the intellectual controversy, but also his firm belief that solutions to archaeological problems lay in fieldwork—a tenet that Haury shared, of course. The archaeological project for which Brew is best known, however, was the excavation centered at the historical-period Hopi pueblo of Awat'ovi and at nearby sites on Antelope Mesa on the Hopi Reservation of northern Arizona. Watson Smith, a prominent member of the Awat'ovi Expedition and fellow of the Peabody Museum, set the tone for 1952 in his *Excavations in Big Hawk Valley*, in which he referred to the Mogollon as a culture of "clouded legitimacy." Characteristically, Brew's students were more outspoken.

In 1952, Hiroshi Daifuku, who had been a student at the Point of Pines Field School in 1948, proposed a "New Conceptual Scheme" for ordering Southwest prehistory. It was a thinly disguised critique of Mogollon distinctiveness, an issue that for most others had been tacitly resolved at the 1948 Pecos Conference. Daifuku's critique originated in his Harvard dissertation on Jeddito 264, a small cluster of pit houses on Antelope Mesa near Awat'ovi, and it echoed the concerns Brew had expressed in his Alkali Ridge report and at the Pecos Conference.

Daifuku (1952:195) concluded "that there has been uncritical acceptance of a concept which has been defined in unworkably absolute terms." His "new conceptual scheme" was a dual configuration of Pueblo and Hohokam, in which both Anasazi and Mogollon were considered Pueblo. The full presentation of Daifuku's argument in *Jeddito 264: A Basket Maker III–Pueblo I Site in Northeastern Arizona* would not be published until 1961. We will return to Jeddito 264 in a subsequent chapter.

At that time, Harvard was a house of independent thinkers. Fred Wendorf's (1953) *Archaeological Studies in the Petrified Forest*—quoted earlier as a summary of the Mogollon controversy—was a Harvard dissertation prepared under Brew and Scott, although the excavation itself was done for and published by the Museum of Northern Arizona. Wendorf reported work at two sites on the Mogollon-Anasazi frontier, addressing questions of taxonomy, culture contact, and blending. Many of his conclusions affirmed Mogollon chronology and fueled arguments for its distinctiveness (Wendorf 2008:64).

Wendorf (1953:160–61) considered the Twin Butte site (White Mound phase, AD 700–900) to closely resemble other Anasazi sites in architecture and ceramics, but there also were resemblances with the Bear Village, particularly in lithic technology. Of the earlier Flattop site, Wendorf (1953:75) wrote, "surprisingly close resemblances are to be noted between this site and the pre-pottery Anasazi of Basket Maker II, the Hilltop Phase of the Bluff Site and somewhat less, the Pine Lawn Phase as represented by the SU Site." The implications were that Mogollon traits could be recognized as early as Basketmaker II times, and basic traits maintained their distinctiveness from Anasazi attributes in what was clearly a mixed or "frontier" area.

The first major publication of the Peabody Museum's Upper Gila Expedition would not be published until 1957. This was E. B. "Ned" Danson's (1957) *An Archaeological Survey of West Central New Mexico and East Central Arizona*. The area selected for survey was a huge chunk of territory in east-central Arizona and west-central New Mexico. Although Danson (1957:30) stated that the reason for selecting this area was because of the relative lack of archaeological work in the region, we suspect that the Upper Gila Expedition did not choose by chance alone to study "the Mogollon, the brown pottery-making people, who had lived in the central mountain belt of Arizona and New Mexico" (Danson 1957:3).

The hundreds of sites discovered during three years of survey formed a powerful database, and in Danson's report, the existence of Mogollon could not be denied. Danson (1957:119) concluded that "One of the results of this survey has been the further strengthening of the theory of the Mogollon Culture." Danson's work also was important in suggesting an ecological, or environmental, basis for differences between Mogollon and Anasazi. "[T]he Mogollon People preferred the mountain country, for their sites were found to be limited to that type of country during the early phases of the Mogollon Culture, and the northern boundary stretched along the northern edge of the central mountain belt." The San Juan Anasazi, by contrast, "preferred to live in the sandy plateau lands rather than the mountain country" (Danson 1957:119). He also provided a topographic explanation—accessibility—for sites showing Anasazi influence.

The second major contribution to emerge from the Upper Gila Expedition appeared in 1962, and it would essentially go unnoticed as a significant piece of scholarship on Southwest prehistory. This was William Bullard's (1962) *The Cerro Colorado Site and Pithouse Architecture in the Southwestern United States Prior to A.D. 900*. Its address of issues surrounding the Mogollon also would be ignored. The monograph was too much, too late, at a moment of rapid and radical change in the development of Southwest archaeology. We discuss Bullard and Cerro Colorado at the end of our story.

Haury had, then, his answer to the question of how the Peabody Museum archaeologists, especially Brew, would tackle the cultural assignment of the sites discovered during the Upper Gila Expedition. Danson would move into the pro-Mogollon camp, whereas Bullard would remain staunchly on the side of the anti-Mogollonists. The reports from the Upper Gila Expedition came after Wheat had produced the definitive synthesis that put an end to the Mogollon controversy. We turn now to how victory was ultimately achieved at Crooked Ridge Village.

Victory at Crooked Ridge

Wheat's doctoral dissertation at the University of Arizona consisted of two parts—a standard site report for Crooked Ridge Village, which we have discussed, and a synthesis of evidence in support of the Mogollon concept as Haury had defined it. The latter was published in 1955 as *Mogollon Culture Prior to A.D. 1000*. According to Wheat (1955:vi), the second part of the study grew out of "the attempt to place Crooked Ridge Village, an early Mogollon site in east-central Arizona, in its proper chronological and cultural context in the Southwest." Wheat defined six branches of Mogollon—San Simon, Mimbres, Black River, Jornada, Cibola, and Forestdale. These were recognized as "regional expressions of culture which, while differing in some details, nevertheless constitute a definite and definable pattern in which the resemblances between areas are greater than the differences" (Wheat 1955:165). Wheat identified a sequence of stages from Mogollon 1 through 5 on the basis of technological criteria other than ceramics and presented a chronology in which Anasazi, Hohokam, and the Mogollon branches were correlated.

Wheat supported his statements concerning the Mogollon culture pattern by examining village pattern (site layout) and architecture, treatment of the dead, pottery, ground stone tools, flaked stone artifacts, bone and antler objects, ornaments, perishable materials, subsistence, and social organization through time (Mogollon 1 through 5) and space (among the six branches).

This work addressed all of the contentious issues surrounding the Mogollon—its antiquity and chronology; relation to the preceramic Cochise, the Anasazi, and the Hohokam; and the priority of Mogollon pottery over Anasazi pottery. Wheat concluded that although some of the traits characterizing Mogollon and Cochise were too generic to be useful in establishing cultural continuity, "others have such detailed resemblances that there can remain little doubt that the late Cochise people of the eastern part of their area became the Mogollon." He supported the Anasazi-swamping theory while dodging a direct confrontation with the post–AD 1000 material.

In the epilogue, Wheat considered all the anti-Mogollon issues that had been raised in previous critiques: Should Mogollon and Hohokam be considered as variants of the same culture pattern? *No.* Should Mogollon and Anasazi be considered as variants of the same culture pattern? *No.* Should Anasazi, Mogollon, Hohokam, and Patayan be considered as separate basic cultures? Although Wheat believed arguing this point was a futile exercise, the answer was a cautious *Yes.*

Unquestionably, Wheat was guided by the taxonomic imperative of culture history, seen in his efforts to classify every piece of Mogollon material culture into types. This framework was not only accepted at the time, it was expected, and as such, the book is a monument to the culture-history approach. Here, gathered together in a single small volume, were all the minutiae hidden in the hundreds of report pages on Mogollon sites and culture. The impact of Wheat's arguments was enhanced by being published as a memoir of *both* the Society for American Archaeology and of the American Anthropological Association. The book's contribution to the Mogollon controversy was that subsequently, no one would feel compelled to submit data to descriptive synthesis in order to prove once again the reality of Mogollon. Except for two monographs to appear in the early sixties, the basic questions of Mogollon distinctiveness and antiquity had been settled.

The argument that Wheat presented rested on and was supported by the prodigious excavation and reporting of Haury, Sayles, Martin, Rinaldo, and Bluhm. Martin would deliver the coup de grace in the Mogollon battle. While Rinaldo was digging Foote Canyon Pueblo in 1955, Martin was planning their move to a new field station in Vernon, Arizona, and writing a book for the Chicago Natural History Museum's Popular Series. It was published in 1959 as *Digging into History: A Brief Account of Fifteen Years of Archaeological Work in New Mexico.* Martin's preface reveals his purpose:

> The purpose of this book is to piece together all the bits of the Mogollon Indian jigsaw puzzle that we discovered in New Mexico in our fifteen years of digging there. We gleaned a lot of odd facts and artifacts during that period, but they begin to shape up a vast and exciting

picture of five thousand years of human history. My hope, here, is to connect these pieces in an orderly manner, and yet to infuse them with at least some of the dynamic overtones we all experienced during these years of discoveries. (Martin 1959a:3)

Martin's descriptive narrative takes the Mogollon from their beginnings in the Chiricahua stage of the preceramic Cochise culture (Sayles and Antevs 1941) through a succession of phases—Pine Lawn, Georgetown, San Francisco, Three Circle, Reserve, Tularosa, Foote Canyon—to the final abandonment of the Pine Lawn Valley–Reserve region sometime between AD 1350 and 1400 (see Martin 1959a:50). In this way, Martin ended the intellectually busy, debate-peppered decade of the 1950s with a concise, readable validation of the Mogollon culture that combined the indigenous development and early distinctiveness of Haury's Mogollon with the post–AD 1000 continuity of Reed's Mogollon into a seamless flow of culture change. In this book, there is not the slightest hint of controversy.

13
Vernon, Arizona, the New Archaeology, and the Mogollon

> I wrote a chapter on our philosophy of education at Vernon
> Field Station. In its conclusion I said "We try to present
> science as an open system, without 'true' or 'right' answers. We
> encourage students to investigate problems, solutions to
> which will help make the complexities of the present as well as
> the prehistoric world—more understandable."
>
> —Paul Sidney Martin (1974:27)

By the beginning of the 1960s, the Mogollon controversy was over for Haury and also for Martin and Rinaldo, the latter duo having moved their field of operation out of New Mexico and into Vernon, Arizona, where a new direction in archaeology would take shape and ultimately spill over into the discipline at large. In the minds of the principals, there were few, if any, loose ends. The Point of Pines field school conducted its last season in 1960 under Thompson's direction, and Haury surely was planning his return to Snaketown, where he would respond to another controversy of interpretation. But at that time, the Peabody Museum of Harvard University cared little about the Hohokam and had much remaining to say about the Mogollon. Indeed, one critique that appeared during this period—William Rotch Bullard's discussion of the Cerro Colorado site and its architecture derived from the Upper Gila Expedition—could have reignited the controversy. A series of unrelated shifts in American archaeology and American universities, however, took center stage and diverted scholarly attention to other, more pressing issues than the Mogollon controversy.

This time was an era of dramatic change in American archaeology, and we see it reflected in Mogollon archaeology in two strikingly disparate approaches. On the one hand, the "new archaeologists" of the Southwest, who rose from the matrix of the Hay Hollow Valley and Martin's

Chicago Natural History Museum field expeditions in Vernon, Arizona, ceased to fiddle with cultural classification and trait lists and transformed the Mogollon into human systems that adapted to their environments. On the other hand, the primary pro-Mogollonists in the earlier battles kept strictly to the culture-history guidelines with which they felt most comfortable. They did fuss a bit over what happened to the Mogollon after AD 1000. Turkey Creek Pueblo at Point of Pines was almost completely excavated during the late 1950s, perhaps in an attempt to investigate Reed's view of the late, pueblo-building Mogollon, and we will explore that possibility later in this chapter.

Before we tackle the dramatic evolution in American archaeology in general and Mogollon archaeology in particular, we turn to Harvard's last stand of the 1960s, a skirmish conducted in the arid plateau country of Arizona and New Mexico.

Harvard's Last Stand on the Colorado Plateau

Two works published just a year apart represented the death throes of Harvard's anti-Mogollon crusade. The first was Daifuku's final, full-text publication of the report on Jeddito 264 in 1961 as a Peabody Museum Paper. In the early 1950s, Daifuku had abstracted some of the points in this work as an initial volley, which we discussed previously. The second and more devastating criticism appeared in 1962 under Bullard's authorship—the report on the Cerro Colorado site.

Antelope Mesa

Jeddito 264 was a village of a half-dozen pit structures and twenty or so masonry storage cists situated on a spur of Antelope Mesa above Jeddito Wash, deep in Hopi country. Nearby in historical times were the Keams Canyon and Jeddito Trading Posts, and the Hopi villages of Awat'ovi, Walpi, and Oraibi crowned the mesa tops. All of these are storied place names in Southwest archaeology. Although Daifuku claimed the monograph to be a site report on a small Basketmaker III–Pueblo I site, he considered only the architecture in detail and reserved a scant thirteen pages, including illustrations, for the artifact assemblage. Instead, the monograph is a critique of the Mogollon culture concept from start to finish. Today, it is almost painful to read the strained conclusions that Daifuku reached in his attempt to discredit the Mogollon.

Daifuku began the report with "The Status of Recent Research in the Southwest." He wrote (Daifuku 1961:10) that although some scholars believed in the distinctiveness of Mogollon, "it has not been universally recognized as having equal taxonomic status with the Pueblo and Hohokam cultures." Daifuku continued:

> The fervor of debate has reached the stage of crusade and counter crusade. The resultant identification of individuals as either pro- or anti-Mogollonists has precluded agreement in the past and will delay agreement for some time to come. The argument boils down to the question of whether to consider the sedentary cultures of the southwestern United States as being bipolar in configuration (Pueblo and Hohokam as dominant cultures) or tripolar (Pueblo, Hohokam, and Mogollon). (Daifuku 1961:10)

In "The Problem of the Pit House," Daifuku reviewed "what is known about the development of the pit house," because "it plays such an important part in the discussion of the status of Mogollon culture" (Daifuku 1961:35). This chapter devoted much effort to tracing pit-house architecture in the Old World and less than one page to Southwest pit structures. Daifuku concluded that pit-house architecture had several common themes, including tendencies to build independent units, to use four roof-support posts, to vary in shape, and to regard the structure as sacred. "On the basis of these considerations it seems that the particular details of Mogollon pit houses are not sufficiently distinct in themselves to support the thesis that they represent a distinctive cultural entity separable from the Pueblo and Hohokam" (Daifuku 1961:45).

One wonders how Daifuku could have reached this conclusion, because he actually offered a great deal of evidence supporting the distinctiveness of Basketmaker III–Pueblo I and Mogollon architecture. Unique to the former were perimeter benches apparently supporting the superstructure, central hearth–ash-pit complexes, low adobe ridges radiating from the hearth–ash-pit complexes, masonry-lined antechambers, partition walls, and separate, slab-lined storage pits. Even a cursory glance at Wheat's *Mogollon Culture* would have demonstrated the absence of these architectural attributes in any Mogollon branch. Only the most fundamental characteristics—circular shape (present only in some areas and periods), quadrilateral roof-support system, and long entries (again present only in some areas and periods)—were shared by Mogollon pit structures and those found at Jeddito 264.

Daifuku did not refer to Wheat's exhaustive trait list, but to Haury's (1936) original suite of traits thought to distinguish the Mogollon. Certainly Wheat's monograph was available to Daifuku, as it was published six years before *Jeddito 264*. The only reference we can find to Wheat 1955 referred to the Western Pueblo complex as the ultimate development from the Mogollon (Daifuku 1961:59), and Wheat 1955 is cited in Daifuku's bibliography. Either Daifuku did not revise the Jeddito 264 manuscript to include Wheat's data or omitted them from the comparison.

Quemado, New Mexico

Cerro Colorado ("Red Hill" in Spanish) is a set of twin buttes near Quemado in west-central New Mexico, a plateau land of sandstone mesas and sandy valleys. Rising some 7,400 ft, the smaller butte commands a sweeping view of the countryside. On the grassy summit ringed with outcrops of basalt, Basketmaker III peoples and those who succeeded them built a hamlet consisting of pit houses, storage structures, ceremonial structures, and storage pits and buried their dead. The thirty-five excavated structures and associated material culture provided the tools for the final dissection of the Mogollon concept. Just as Daifuku had done with Jeddito 264, Bullard seems to have used the site report as an excuse for an essentially unrelated critique.

In *The Cerro Colorado Site and Pithouse Architecture in the Southwestern United States Prior to A.D. 900*, also a Peabody Museum Paper, Bullard reflected a subtle change in the form of criticism leveled at the Mogollon. Whereas early critiques attempted to deny its existence—a denial too anachronistic for the decade in which Bullard wrote—he concentrated instead on a demolition of its chronology through the mechanism of intricate and tedious ceramic reevaluations. In spite of some well-placed observations on the dating of Tularosa Cave and Crooked Ridge Village and misinterpretation of the Pine Lawn phase at the SU site, Bullard was unable to shake loose the Hilltop phase in the Forestdale Valley from its tree-ring-dated position around AD 300. Bullard concluded his review of Mogollon and Hohokam dating with the statement that "It is hard to avoid the conclusion that many of the difficulties which we experience with the chronology of these areas are the result of attempts to give the regional sequences of the Mogollon culture comparatively great antiquity so as to conform, directly or indirectly, with the original estimated Snaketown dating" (Bullard 1962:93).

Bullard then turned to a comparison of pit-house architecture across the Southwest as equally detailed as the ceramic comparisons, if not more so. Bullard defined a Peripheral and a Nuclear Mogollon Area and concluded: "Equally as important as the need for more excavation is the need for continual re-appraisals of older concepts in the light of new data. Recent interpretations of Mogollon archaeology, in particular, suffer from failure to make such re-appraisals as well as to take into account the factors of regional variation" (Bullard 1962:190).

Bullard's critique has been widely cited but never fully evaluated. Perhaps Martin's response to the opportunity to review Bullard's monograph for *American Antiquity* is indicative of its impact upon advocates of Mogollon, especially those like Martin, whose work Bullard had criticized so severely. Martin turned the task over to his top graduate student—William Longacre—who would become a prominent figure in the soon-to-explode "New Archaeology." We can view this transfer from Martin to Longacre as symbolic of what was to happen to investigations of the Mogollon as a result of changes in archaeology.

American archaeology in the 1960s embarked on a quest to develop scientific method and theory appropriate to understanding the sociology and ecology of past peoples, regardless of their cultural affiliation or particular history. Concerns with culture history and cultural affiliation became unfashionable, even low-brow, archaeology. For example, McGregor's 1965 edition of his textbook, *Southwestern Archaeology*, was reorganized into prehistoric *periods*, rather than the *cultures* that had structured his original 1941 book, the one that so inflamed Brew.

Within this academic regime change, Bullard's punctilious reevaluation of pit-house chronology may have been lost, regardless of contributing factors of person and place. Bullard was a Mayanist, and, according to Gordon R. Willey's portrait, had always been a Mayanist who just happened to have spent two summers on the Upper Gila Expedition. Willey—a Harvard faculty member famed for his pioneering work in settlement patterns of ancient Peru—wrote, "while [Bullard] was working with me in British Honduras, he also spent two summers (1953 and 1954) in the Southwestern United States as Jo Brew's assistant. The results of this Southwestern fieldwork were developed as a doctoral dissertation at the same time he was concerning himself with Maya settlement patterns" (Willey 1988:320). Concerning Bullard's dissertation, Willey wrote:

As might be expected of Bill, it is a lucid field account; but it goes beyond this in a section entitled "A Review and Critique of Anasazi, Mogollon, and Hohokam Chronology Prior to AD 900." In this, he displays that very clear writing which flowed from his clear thinking. He tackled, and I think he successfully answered, many of the questions that were then besetting Southwestern archaeologists about the nature and ancestry of Mogollon culture. (Willey 1988:335)

Another indicator of Bullard's prominence in the Harvard academic community, in addition to Willey's portrait, is that he was invited to serve as the Peabody Museum's assistant director to Brew, a position he held from 1963 to 1968. According to Willey (1988:334), "[Bullard] proved to be a conscientious and effective assistant director. He liked curatorial work and was good at it. He promoted orderliness in the Museum's collection storage, and he also set up some small exhibits. By more recent standards, Bill would be called pretty conservative when it came to display installations." As assistant director, he was probably thoroughly involved in the planning and execution of the Peabody Museum's one hundredth birthday celebration on October 8, 1966 (Brew 1968). Unfortunately, Bullard died relatively early in his career, in 1972, at the age of forty-five.

Had Bullard been a southwestern archaeologist and not a Mayanist, had he not been consumed by museum curatorial duties immediately after the publication of his penetrating critique of Mogollon chronology, and had he not died at an early age, then the Mogollon controversy may have sputtered along, even though the discipline as a whole was rapidly shifting away from a focus on questions of chronology, cultural taxonomy, and affiliation. Bullard raised serious issues concerning critical points of interpretation, the answers to which would have added considerable refinements to our understanding of the nature and development of Mogollon culture.

Vernon, Arizona, and the Genesis of the New Archaeology

As questions of culture process came to dominate those of culture history, concern with the Mogollon as a culture and its relationship to other cultures on a broad time-space scale receded into the background. Investigations of social organization and adaptation of inhabitants at individual sites and of population dynamics and settlement-subsistence systems in thoroughly surveyed areas rose to prominence. The Mogollon "culture" was rarely mentioned in the literature, and then only to anchor one's site or area to the traditional framework of Southwest prehistory. We can relate this shift, at least in part, to the establishment of Martin's field expedition at Vernon, Arizona, and to the rising stars of the new archaeology who worked there.

In 1956, Martin moved the expedition to Vernon, Arizona, a small town in the piñon-juniper woodlands on the fringes of the Colorado Plateau. From there, he would launch surveys and excavations that would add greatly to our understanding of Mogollon prehistory. It was also at Vernon that the transformation of Mogollon culture in the hands of the new archaeologists took place.

Why did Martin move the field camp from Reserve, New Mexico, where it had been located for fifteen seasons, to Vernon? An answer comes from the third monograph from the Vernon expedition, the report on the Mineral Creek site and Hooper Ranch Pueblo. Martin explained:

> [W]e were eager to find out where the Mogollon Indians moved to, why they emigrated, and what became finally of the cultural elements that they had developed. Did these elements disappear, leaving no traces? Or had they been passed on to other groups, and if so, would we able to detect them? Had Mogollon influences filtered into the Zuni area or had Mogollon people themselves left their ancient homeland in the mountains of western New Mexico and migrated in to the Zuni region proper? (Martin 1961:3)

Investigating the Mogollon continuity issue may also have been important to Martin. He also stated (Martin 1961:3–4) that "Mogollon or Mogollon-like traits" had become established in the upper Little Colorado River drainage as early as AD 900, and correlations between the later Mogollon sites of the Pine Lawn–Reserve area and the twelfth-through fourteenth-century pueblos of the upper Little Colorado region were readily recognized. Fuel for an argument of continuity between the pre–AD 1000 and post–AD 1000 Mogollon is certainly apparent in Martin's statement.

Seeds of greater change in Mogollon archaeology came in 1959, when a new archaeologist joined the Vernon field crew—Longacre, then a graduate student at the University of Chicago. That summer, he conducted a survey covering more than three hundred square miles, locating 107 sites

(Martin, Rinaldo, and Longacre 1961:148). More importantly, Longacre would shortly leave an indelible imprint on Southwest archaeology.

The following season (1960) at Vernon was distinctive for several reasons. The National Science Foundation provided funds that supported archaeological survey, palynological analysis, and excavation of a preceramic site. Constance Cronin and Leslie G. Freeman Jr., joined the expedition staff. In the report of the season's work (Martin et al. 1962), Freeman presented a statistical analysis of painted pottery, and Cronin discussed ceramic design elements, both of which were innovations that would come to characterize many subsequent processual studies. The pollen analyses also set the tone for subsequent studies in delineating environmental shifts that spurred abandonment and population movement.

In 1961, the Chicago archaeologists excavated Carter Ranch Pueblo near Snowflake, Arizona. Although Rinaldo reported on this unprepossessing site of about forty rooms in the usual descriptive fashion (Martin et al. 1962), Longacre would launch ceramic sociology from this platform, building the initial reports in the Martin et al. volume into a fully fledged dissertation subsequently published as the University of Arizona Anthropological Paper *Archaeology as Anthropology: A Case Study* (Longacre 1970).

The fruit of these labors was a concern with settlement patterns, adaptive processes, and Mogollon *systems*, not the Mogollon *culture*. This is perhaps best exemplified in Martin's discussion of the Mogollon in *The Archaeology of Arizona* (Martin and Plog 1973). In the chapter on "Adaptation of Man to the Mountains," Martin wrote that it was necessary "to speak briefly of the Mogollon culture and point out why it is merely a subsystem of Southwestern culture and not a distinct and independent cultural entity within the Southwestern system" (Martin and Plog 1973:180). In Martin's view, all ancient southwestern systems were organized in much the same way, but functional and structural differences arose as a result of the adaptation to the environment—in the case of the Mogollon, to the mountainous, cool, well-watered country of east-central Arizona and west-central New Mexico.

In the 1960s, the debate over Mogollon legitimacy was essentially over, and the new Mogollon archaeologists were developing fresh paradigms. Certain questions of Mogollon culture history lingered, however. As late as 1965, even those who were convinced of the reality and substance of Mogollon remained a house divided between those who believed in Anasazi, or Ancestral Pueblo, amalgamation and those who leaned toward

Reed's Western Pueblo model. Reed's pueblo-building Mogollon of the post–AD 1000 period had been the subject of the 1951 Pecos Conference symposium held at Point of Pines. Two of the premier Mogollon scholars would address the issue, as we discuss next.

Western Pueblo Redux

By the end of the decade, Martin joined Reed in believing in continuity between the pre–AD 1000 and post–AD 1000 Mogollon. His arguments for continuity were made in prose. Haury would argue the issue as he always did, with the shovel, by leading the Point of Pines field school in the excavation of Turkey Creek Pueblo.

Pine Lawn Valley, New Mexico

In his *Digging into History*, Martin (1959a) wrote a final chapter on "The Beginnings of Town Life, About A.D. 1000 to A.D. 1350." He affirmed Mogollon continuity throughout the presentation by referring to "Mogollon Indians," "Mogollon people," "Mogollon towns," "Mogollon development," and possible factors responsible for cultural change. Martin was justifiably compelled to tackle the thorny issue of radical cultural change while sparing the general reader any mention of the academic controversy surrounding this once-touchy subject. Without committing himself to any particular process of change, he provided the general reader and the academic skeptic with ample causes of change to explore in their own minds, writing:

> Innovations are frequently brought about when habitual ways of doing things are discouraged and when a significant event occurs that changes the situation to which a people have become accustomed. Some such significant alterations of life conditions may be: (1) an increase in population; (2) a change in climate; (3) a migration into a new environment; (4) contacts (by trade or war) with other people; (5) catastrophes, such as floods or droughts, crop failure, epidemics, or wars; (6) discoveries of new techniques; and (7) the rise of a powerful leader. (Martin 1959a:104–6)

In a very real sense, Martin completed the Mogollon publication onslaught that marked the latter half of the 1950s and set the tone for the 1960s. He summarized for the general reader and the student fifteen years of Mogollon fieldwork and site reports in the Pine Lawn Valley; testified to his belief in cultural continuity from the Archaic period Chiricahua stage of the Cochise culture to the Mogollon abandonment of the valley; and provided possible reasons for culture change to satisfy those who might raise an objection to his change of heart in seeing the same Mogollon changing from pit houses to pueblos. Haury, of course, would take a different approach to the continuity problem at Point of Pines.

Turkey Creek Pueblo

The excavation of Turkey Creek Pueblo (AZ W:9:123) under the supervision of Alfred E. Johnson, then a graduate student at the University of Arizona, was Haury's last excavation toward resolving the question he had selected as the topic of the 1951 Pecos Conference at Point of Pines—Mogollon amalgamation or continuity in the period after AD 1000. Readers will recall that the original model of Mogollon cultural development ended at that time, when the Mogollon were thought to have been assimilated by the pueblo-building, white-ware-making Anasazi, or Ancestral Pueblo.

Turkey Creek Pueblo is a rarity in the annals of southwestern archaeology for the thoroughness of excavation and the speed with which it was accomplished. During the three field-school seasons of 1958 through 1960, 314 pueblo rooms of an estimated total of 335 were excavated (Haury 1989; Lowell 1991). In addition, the excavation of exterior trash mounds uncovered more than 300 human burials. Most of this work was accomplished by Apache workmen supported by a grant from the National Science Foundation. Haury, writing when well into his eighties, was unequivocal in his views of the inhabitants' cultural affiliation:

> The builders of Turkey Creek village were, indeed, Anasazi, who lived in the southern frontier of their range. They introduced the concept of pueblo architecture into the region, where a local tradition of pit house dwelling held sway. The Nantack Village of pit houses was immediately antecedent to Turkey Creek Pueblo and it, or the time it represents, is viewed as the end of Mogollon dominance in the Point of Pines area. (Haury 1989:100–102)

Johnson's 1965 dissertation topic probably would have been a site report for Turkey Creek Pueblo, had he not been assigned to assist William W. Wasley of the Arizona State Museum in the salvage archaeology at

Painted Rocks Reservoir (Wasley and Johnson 1965). Instead, Johnson (1965) examined the development of Western Pueblo culture, on the surface a triumphant affirmation of Reed's concept. Johnson, however, redefined Western Pueblo to be a syncretism or amalgamation of Mogollon, Anasazi, and Hohokam features, which submerged the old Mogollon in a new cultural entity. Reed's original concept and definition thus changed meaning in the hands of those who would see Mogollon as swamped. In another curious twist to the story, Johnson would go on to teach at the University of Kansas, returning to the sweeping plains that Haury had left in 1925.

Martin reversed his position on Anasazi swamping of Mogollon (Martin and Plog 1973). We mention this only as a curiosity that might be attributed to any one of several personal factors, such as declining health or advancing age, an ideological change of heart, or new political and social alliances forged in Martin's sunset years. Regardless, in the systems-rich *Archaeology of Arizona*, Martin (Martin and Plog 1973:194) explained the Anasazi swamping theory in terms of ecological systems: "'[I]f two or more different kinds of sociocultural systems occupy adjacent environmental zones, the one that can be altered or adapted to fit the adjacent environmental zone will expand at the expense of the resident system' (the Mogollon, in this case)." As Anasazi communities grew and expanded into the Mogollon region, "for all intents and purposes the Mogollon area after AD 1000 became an Anasazi one." In Martin and Plog's book, the upper Little Colorado River pueblos that Martin and crew had excavated were grouped with Chaco, Mesa Verde, and others as Anasazi.

But even as these paradigm and ideological shifts were taking place, the pillars of the Mogollon remained true to their cultural-historical ideals. This is seen best in the Pecos Conference of 1967, which was held in hot and steamy Tucson, Arizona.

The Pecos Conference, Tucson, Arizona, 1967

Some forty years after Kidder convened the first one, the thirtieth Pecos Conference was held in Tucson on August 25 and 26, 1967, which any Tucson resident knows is a horrible time to be in that city, when the monsoons typically add high humidity to the 100-degree-plus temperatures. The scheduled symposium, organized by the program chair William J. Robinson, was "The Mogollon Today" and was chaired by Reed.

Although no transcript of the session exists, the topics and speakers indicate the range of issues presented, or using a more appropriate metaphor, the "hymns sung by the choir." Nonbelievers were conspicuously absent from the program, but the reader should keep in mind that this was Tucson in August. We rely once more on Richard Woodbury's (1993:299–300) research when discussing the Pecos Conference as well as an informal lunch interview with Robinson. "The Mogollon Today" symposium had the following program:

> The Mogollon Pattern: Joe Ben Wheat
> The Mogollon Tree-Ring Chronology: William J. Robinson
> Northern Mogollon: John B. Rinaldo
> Hohokam-Mogollon Relationships: Emil W. Haury
> Early Horizons in the Navajo Reservoir: A. E. Dittert Jr.
> Southern Mogollon: Charles C. Di Peso
> Early Horizons in the Puerco-Hopi Buttes Area: George
>   J. Gumerman
> Mogollon Agriculture: Mark P. Leone
> Summary: Erik K Reed

Prior to lunching with Robinson, we were certain that the Pecos Conference symposium was in response to Bullard's 1962 attack on the Mogollon and Hohokam chronologies. We were itching to hear Robinson confirm this belief. Robinson, who had been the program chair for that conference and originator of the symposium, could not recall Bullard even being mentioned, and that the reason for the conference was the redating of important Mogollon sites by the Laboratory of Tree-Ring Research.

Beginning in 1963 with National Science Foundation support, the Laboratory of Tree-Ring Research at the University of Arizona began a comprehensive reanalysis of its archaeological tree-ring specimens from southwestern sites. The reanalysis progressed according to the Arizona State Museum quadrangles for designating sites, each quad being one degree of latitude by one degree of longitude and given an alphabetic label by state. By 1966, four quadrangle reports had been published: Arizona K (Puerco–Wide Ruin–Ganado Area), Arizona E (Chinle–De Chelly–Red Rock Area), and Arizona N, O, P, Q (Verde–Showlow–St. Johns Area). The P quad contained the important Forestdale Valley pithouse villages of Bluff and Bear. The New Mexico S quad had also been completed by the time of the Pecos Conference, as attested by Robinson's two-page handout with tree-ring dates and ceramic data on pit houses from SU, Harris Village, Mogollon Village, Turkey Foot Ridge, Stark-weather, and Wheatley Ridge.

At last, Mogollon had been dated by a scientifically valid, absolute technique and shown to be as early in the Pine Lawn Valley (SU site) as it was in the Forestdale Valley (Bluff Village). The Mogollon pit-house chronology was unassailable, and that may be a reason Bullard's analysis was not a topic of discussion at this conference.

Because of the radical redirection in American archaeology and, perhaps also, of the exhaustion engendered by the protracted controversy surrounding the authenticity and antiquity of Mogollon, many of the interesting questions raised during the controversy and the major features of Mogollon culture and behavior remained essentially unresolved. Throughout the period of the "New Archaeology," no one paid much attention to the Mogollon. This would change dramatically when archaeologists working under the Behavioral Archaeology banner at Grasshopper Pueblo and scholars studying other Mogollon communities rediscovered the signal importance of culture.

14
Personality and Place in Prehistory

> For most, it is remembered as one of the richest experiences
> of their lives. This can only mean that the environment in which
> we lived, the atmosphere of the camp, and the circumjacent
> archaeological advantages offered the ideal combination of
> elements favorable for a meaningful learning experience. If
> the reader catches a feeling of these qualities in this account,
> then its purpose will have been well served.
>
> —Emil Haury (1989:xv)

The Mogollon controversy had ended in 1955, for all intents and purposes, with Wheat's extraordinary tour de force, *Mogollon Culture Prior
to A.D. 1000*. There would be a few minor resurgences as the Harvard
contingent refused to concede defeat, but the controversy would never
achieve the scale and importance that it assumed during the 1940s. It
would be implausible to imagine that Wheat accomplished the happy
ending to the Mogollon controversy alone, although his subsequent,
successful career in southwestern archaeology would give credence to
such a claim. Instead, we are convinced, it was Haury's strategic intellect
that fostered a rather complicated series of academic and logistical moves
designed to end the controversy. To that, we add the intangible variables
of personality as they operated within the unique structure of place.
Resolving the Mogollon controversy involved a perfect concatenation of
academic power, intellectual force, strategic thinking, and strong personalities, nurtured in the unique landscape of Point of Pines. In this
chapter, we summarize the forces that molded an academic and intellectual controversy that cast long shadows in the annals of Southwest
archaeology and discuss its equally significant closure.

The Power of Place

We believe strongly in the power of place to mold individuals, cultures, and entire nations. As we have discussed, people construct cultural landscapes by means of their interactions with the biological and physical environments and other humans. In turn, we are shaped by the forces of the natural and social environments, often profoundly. Place was a vital factor in the Mogollon controversy on many different levels. The first place to affect Haury was the landscape of his youth, where his personality and intellect were molded. The flat, stark plains of Kansas—a place where, as Willa Cather observed of New Mexico, the earth was the floor of the sky—grew stalwart men and women, and in the close community of Bethel College, intellectual pursuits, a simple lifestyle, faith, and hard labor merged to nurture the young man who ventured to Cuicuilco in 1925. Surely this background developed Haury's abilities to cope with controversy and the vicissitudes of academic life. Just as surely, it shaped an epistemology that was rooted in the scientific method and positivist thought.

Haury next encountered the Southwest, a mosaic of green pines, dissected mountains, red sandstone cliffs, and thorny desert so different from the Kansas plains of his boyhood. Its diversity of terrain and landscape features could scarcely be ignored, nor could its impacts on ancient peoples be dismissed. Here, we think, Haury's innate romanticism—a personality characteristic that is well hidden in his professional writings, but which comes through clearly in the bits and pieces of the family archives—could flourish. Only a few easterners can encounter the Southwest's vast skies and cloudscapes; its pungent smells of creosote, rain on hot stone, and wood smoke; its native peoples, and not be changed irrevocably. We think the Southwest landscape must have drawn Haury as it has done us, and its remarkable diversity offered a canvas on which to sketch notions of ancient cultures that could be explored in the field. We also think it must have tested Haury, as the Southwest tests all, and his personality and abilities not only enabled him to cope with the environmental and cultural challenges but allowed his scholarship to flourish.

Of all the places in Haury's life, we believe Point of Pines was the most remarkable and the most significant to Haury emotionally and personally. We have mentioned that the choice of Point of Pines as the field on which to play out the battle for the Mogollon was not accidental. The decision to move the University of Arizona Archaeological Field

School to Point of Pines was made for a bundle of reasons we have discussed, not the least of which was to continue to argue the Mogollon concept with the shovel. Haury knew that the many ruins in the Point of Pines region would not only provide firsthand survey and excavation experience for the field-school students. These ruins also represented the plain-brown-ware-making, pit-house-dwelling people of the mountains he had first named the Mogollon. Haury's experience in the Forestdale Valley no doubt alerted him to the possibility that Anasazi peoples had lived alongside the Mogollon, and he may have intuited that Point of Pines would be an excellent laboratory to study the so-called swamping of the Mogollon by puebloan peoples after AD 1000. As he recalled (Haury 1979:228), "the area was ideal to view the merging of Mogollon and Anasazi and the consequent effects of that phenomenon." Point of Pines was a place "where a correlation of the histories of the Pueblo, Hohokam, and Mogollon could be made, if this were possible anywhere" (Haury 1950b:7).

Here we must mention one facet of the process of doing archaeology that seldom comes to mind, although cultural anthropologists have considered it (e.g., Royce 2002). This is the experience of being in the field and how this experience shapes archaeological interpretations (Scheiber 2008). We remember our field experiences fondly (e.g., Haury 1989; McGregor 1987; Reid and Whittlesey 2005), but few have investigated their field experiences with an anthropologist's eye. When we think about the intersection of place and personality, we must consider the reflexive nature of Haury's seasonal migration to a summer camp in a place so distinct from his Sonoran Desert home the rest of the year, but to which he returned year after year. The daily rhythms of camp life and archaeological investigation surely shaped Haury's interpretations "at the trowel's edge," as Hodder (2003) has expressed it. The isolated and circumscribed archaeological field camp at Point of Pines became a layered landscape of social memory, where the daily tasks the group carried out, their interactions with the San Carlos Apache, and the daily and deep intersections with the land resulted in shared social meanings that embodied the values, attitudes, and core beliefs of the archaeologists.

The Point of Pines region would prove more archaeologically productive than even Haury had anticipated. Within its borders, archaeologists would discover sites suitable for providing answers to almost every Mogollon question then posed, and more. This bucolic mountain island, a grassy plateau watered by springs and winter snows, attracted many different peoples in prehistory, and the traces of their passing on the rocky land left a vast store of information for archaeologists to discover. The first site the archaeologists excavated was a twenty-one-room pueblo— AZ W:10:51, a site "too small to name." It provided a good example of the last phase of occupation of the Point of Pines region, and because it was on the western flank of AZ W:10:50, the huge Point of Pines Pueblo, it represented the beginning of the multiseason campaign at that site. Site AZ W:10:51 had further value—it demonstrated an earlier occupation predating the late pueblo that bore the hallmarks of the Mogollon (Wendorf 1950). It also confirmed that the "long history of contact between the Mogollon and the Anasazi" established at Forestdale Valley was present at Point of Pines, where it may have "tended to blur the sharper distinctions which may have existed between the two cultures prior to these contacts" (Wendorf 1950:114).

In subsequent years, field-school students and staff extended their explorations of Mogollon culture through the entire occupational sequence of the Point of Pines region. At the Cienega Creek site (AZ W:10:112), they defined a Middle and Late Archaic period occupation that strengthened the notion that the Mogollon culture developed from Cochise culture roots (Haury 1957).

Without question, the pre–AD 1000 Mogollon sites figured prominently. The most critical of these was Crooked Ridge Village, the Mogollon pit-house site where Haury planned a multiseason excavation and that he used as the centerpiece for the 1948 and 1951 Pecos Conferences held at Point of Pines. As we have seen, it was Crooked Ridge Village that provided primary data for ending the Mogollon controversy.

Nantack Village (AZ W:10:111) offered a glimpse of the last phase of occupation before surface pueblos were constructed in the region, what Breternitz (1959:1) described as a poorly understood time in the Point of Pines chronology. Ten excavated residential structures and a great kiva— the largest excavated to date at that time—provided material to define the Nantack phase, and six excavated surface-masonry rooms informed on the later Reserve and Tularosa phases. Haury (1989:80) expressed the fact that the site was interesting because it was "a blending of Mogollon and Anasazi attributes," and the beginning of what "some scholars have referred to as the Anasazi take-over or 'swamping' of the Mogollon people." For Haury, Nantack Village represented a crucial moment when the blending of the two groups was beginning to take shape.

The pueblo ruins of the later phases gave insights into unexpected but highly significant issues. The big ruin of Point of Pines Pueblo (AZ w:10:50), where excavations were begun in the 1947 season, would offer evidence of an extraordinary event in Southwest prehistory—a migration of Anasazi peoples from the Kayenta-Tusayan region of Arizona in the late AD 1200s. Haury (1958) reported the unfortunate end to this intriguing story. Excavations there would also reveal an astonishing great kiva, among other serendipitous finds. Chance also played a role, if minor, at Point of Pines.

Investigations into the water- and soil-control features of the region yielded information concerning the Mogollon people's masterly control of floodwater and dry farming. Check dams were built into the smaller drainages, and stone alignments spread the water onto the fields. Catchment basins, or reservoirs, and walk-in wells supplied domestic water (Wheat 1952; Woodbury 1961).

Finally, the location of Point of Pines on the San Carlos Apache Reservation provided a tantalizing prospect of linking the abandonment of the area by its prehistoric inhabitants with the arrival of the Western Apache. Haury (1950b:8) wrote, "The question which came to mind concerned the role played by the Apache in their expansion into what was formerly Pueblo territory. Was there physical contact between these divergent peoples? If so, when? And what were the consequences? Or, if the abandonment of the area by the Pueblos and the immigration by the Apache were independent of each other, what was the cause of the former event?" James C. Gifford would tackle this problem in *Archaeological Explorations in the Caves of the Point of Pines Region, Arizona* (1980), along with Asch (1961), who discussed Willow Creek Pueblo, where Apache wickiups were built over the ruined pueblo rooms.

Important although it was, the rich archaeological record was not Point of Pines' sole attraction. Haury's deep feelings for this special place are revealed in many contexts, not the least of which is his personal memoir of the field school (Haury 1989), and although he wrote of Point of Pines in his characteristically sparse style, the reader knows the heartfelt emotions that lie between the words and the lines. He always hoped the field school would return to Point of Pines; it was his center place, his spiritual and intellectual home.

The Importance of Personality: Archaeologists and Debate

Whereas place provided the primacy of context for Haury's argument, it was the force of his own personality and his strategic design that would structure the debate. We can see this illustrated well in Haury's hosting of two Pecos Conferences at Point of Pines to discuss Mogollon issues and to illustrate the Mogollon archaeological record in the ground. Two features of this move stand out in our minds. Clearly, archaeological arguments within the culture-history paradigm were most powerful and convincing when prominent scholars were able to view the remains first-hand, in place, in the field, and Haury structured these conferences to make this form of argument. As he stated many times, argument by shovel was his preferred dialectic, one that he employed in clarifying Hohokam issues as well as in the Mogollon controversy.

Haury's recollections underscore these points. Regarding the 1948 Pecos Conference, he recalled:

> The question of the Mogollon Culture was high on the Conference's agenda. Joe Ben Wheat, one of the advanced students, was assigned the task of investigating the Crooked Ridge Village, an impressive place with many early pit houses and residual cultural materials which were clearly related to what we had seen in the Forestdale Valley and in the Mogollon and Harris villages of New Mexico. He had made excellent progress on the project during the summer. We saw Crooked Ridge Village as testimony of the Mogollon people's primacy in the long story of Point of Pines archaeology. The advantage of in-depth discussion during the Conference was to be in a setting where much Mogollon history took place. In addition to talking, we could go out and see the evidence. Crooked Ridge made an impressive display. (Haury 1979:171–72)

More impressive to us and not apparent to those who have never run a field school in the central mountains of Arizona is the extreme logistical nightmare of putting on these two conferences, especially at the end of a long, arduous field season. Having experienced the physical and mental exhaustion of more than twenty field-school seasons, we know the heroic efforts required to host a major, regional conference and understand why Haury's 1989 reflections on these conferences focus more on the meals served than on the issues discussed. One has to travel the old road from San Carlos to Point of Pines to appreciate fully the difficulty of access and then imagine doing it during the August rainy season. The two Pecos Conferences held at Point of Pines represent powerful motivations on Haury's part to persuade his colleagues that his Mogollon concept was workable as well as necessary.

Perhaps the cleverest of Haury's strategies was to choose Wheat as the graduate student in charge of the Crooked Ridge Village work for his dissertation research. Haury had newly installed a doctoral program in anthropology at the University of Arizona, and Wheat would be the second product in 1953, falling alphabetically after Charles Di Peso. Wheat's dissertation also included a Mogollon literature review, or, more appropriately, a synthesis of what was known and claimed about Mogollon up to that time. Wheat's dissertation would be published in a variety of pieces and places, setting a publishing record that would never again be duplicated in American archaeology.

The first publication was a summary titled "Southwestern Cultural Interrelationships and the Question of Area Co-tradition" (Wheat 1954b) in a special Southwest issue of the *American Anthropologist* that Haury organized and edited. Wheat's neophyte status stands out in a symposium composed of the day's most prominent southwestern scholars—Ralph Beals, Brew, Paul Kirchhoff, Kluckhohn, Kroeber, Martin, Reed, Irving Rouse, Carl Sauer, Watson Smith, Edward Spicer, Taylor, Ruth Underhill, and Willey, to name a few. Comments on Wheat's paper by Brew and Smith (1954:586–88) noted that it was actually about the Mogollon.

Wheat's second dissertation-derived publication was the site report for Crooked Ridge Village, which was issued in 1954 as a University of Arizona *Bulletin* (Wheat 1954a). It was the third publication, however, that set the all-time record and illustrates Haury's academic power within the American anthropological community. *Mogollon Culture Prior to A.D. 1000* was published in 1955 both as a Memoir of the American Anthropological Association and a Memoir of the Society for American Archaeology, which meant that every professional archaeologist in the United States got one and probably two copies of Wheat's Mogollon literature review and synthesis, in addition, of course, to the earlier summary article in *American Anthropologist*. This publication avalanche by a fresh PhD has never been duplicated in American archaeology, and we doubt that it ever will be. The uniqueness of this publication feat, though circumstantial, is sufficient for us to credit Haury with being the master player whose hand also is evident in more subtle areas.

Not immediately apparent in the Mogollon controversy and its seeming resolution in the late 1950s is the relationship of the Mogollon chronology to the emerging controversy over the Hohokam chronology. As critiqued by Bullard (1962), Wheat's interpretation of the Crooked Ridge Village chronology was closely tied to the validation of the original Hohokam chronology that Haury developed (Gladwin et al. 1937).

Part of the maneuvering, therefore, to resolve the Mogollon controversy anticipated the upcoming Hohokam controversy that would focus hardest on the chronology and ultimately force Haury to mount his second excavation at the site of Snaketown in 1964 and 1965. There is some irony in this situation. No sooner had Haury masterfully orchestrated a successful conclusion to the Mogollon controversy than another one began to consume his research energy.

Other personalities played important roles in the overall Mogollon controversy. Although Reed's contribution to its resolution was minor compared to Wheat's, we believe that his Western Pueblo concept divided the Mogollon controversy into two parts that could be treated separately—pit-house villagers and pueblo builders. Certainly that is what Wheat did in capping his review at AD 1000, the point when the pit-house building Mogollon switched to aboveground pueblos, and not coincidentally, also avoiding a conflict with his dissertation adviser. This bifurcation of the controversy eased Wheat's review task as well as made acceptance of the pit-house Mogollon more palatable to those needing to be convinced. Here we cannot escape the relevance of place in shaping the personalities of the players in the Mogollon controversy, a topic we will return to in another section.

The strongest piece of evidence in our argument—that it was Haury's personality and academic stature that allowed closure of the Mogollon controversy, along with the rich database found at Point of Pines—is a virtually unknown, seldom-cited doctoral dissertation by James Ball Shaeffer. Titled *The Mogollon Complex: Its Cultural Role and Historical Development in the American Southwest*, the dissertation was submitted to the faculty of Columbia University in 1954. Shaeffer selected the particular problem of the Mogollon culture at the urging of Julian H. Steward, according to his acknowledgments. Steward was chairman of the anthropology department and a prominent scholar of Great Basin tribes and in what came to be known as cultural ecology. It is intriguing that like Reed, Steward also spent time at the avant-garde Deep Springs school, where he, too, must have developed a fascination with the high deserts of the Great Basin. Shaeffer also cited the advice and encouragement of William Duncan Strong, Kroeber, and Richard Woodbury, and most tellingly, thanked Brew and Watson Smith for taking the time to read and comment on his manuscript. Shaeffer first presented the "background to the Mogollon problem," in which the twin issues of Mogollon validity and antiquity are set forth. Noting that the Mogollon data were carried up to that time in archaeologists' heads, Shaeffer (1954:3) proposed: "The historical and cultural role of Mogollon in the Southwest will be supported, therefore, by a detailed tabular analysis of all the Mogollon data, together with a somewhat less detailed summary of Anasazi and Hohokam data." He took a historical, typological, functional, and regional approach to data presentation. If this sounds familiar, it should. It was the identical structure of Wheat's dissertation. What is so striking, however, is the diametrically opposite conclusion at which Shaeffer arrived.

Shaeffer wrote:

> If the culture of the Mogollon area is claimed to be unique or distinctive compared with that of the Anasazi or Hohokam areas, this fact does not appear to be demonstrated by the distributional analysis of its technical or cultural development. Technologically, almost all traits found in the Mogollon area are duplicated elsewhere in the Southwest; culturally, activities of the Mogollon area are practiced through the Southwest. Although regional differences do appear in the Mogollon material, they are mainly typological differences which effect [sic] the superficial appearance of the artifacts, not differences which show initially diverse traditions or attitudes or ways of living. Therefore, if typological differences principally distinguish the Mogollon from the Anasazi and Hohokam material, then Mogollon is a regional variation of a generalized pattern. (Shaeffer 1954:36)

Shaeffer then compared and contrasted flaked stone tools, ground stone tools, bone tools, pottery, burial practices, cranial deformation, architecture, perishable materials, and shell ornaments among Mogollon, Hohokam, and Anasazi. He also discussed "economic and social activities," under which he included agriculture, hunting, ornamentation, manufacturing, warfare, and religion. He finished with a study of the direction of diffusion through which the Mogollon received a considerable number of traits from the Hohokam. Shaeffer's conclusions were:

> (1) major traits in the Mogollon area, excepting lithic survivals, are mainly Hohokam, augmented by those of Anasazi and Mogollon origin; (2) Mogollon tradition is characterized mainly by the development of distinctive typological variations which early become Anasazi influenced and later almost Anasazi submerged; (3) the Mogollon tradition is not a basic undeveloped trait pattern but one of the weaker stylistic traditions or typological complexes within the Southwestern Culture Area. (Shaeffer 1954:1)

To be fair, Shaeffer (1954:i) acknowledged that the research and writing of his dissertation was extended over a period of about five years, largely due to military duty and other responsibilities. Certainly Shaeffer did not have a Crooked Ridge Village to provide supportive data; the research was based entirely on the literature. But that, too, was lacking, as Shaeffer did not cite Wheat, although there is a 1953 citation to Fred Wendorf's review of Martin and his colleagues' work at Tularosa and Cordova Caves. The contrast between Wheat's work and Shaeffer's work is extraordinary. We leave it to the reader to decide whether Haury's influence was the decisive factor in the difference. Perhaps ironically, in 1946, Shaeffer became the caretaker of Kinishba Ruin, the Mogollon Pueblo ruin on the Fort Apache Indian Reservation that Cummings had excavated and reconstructed in the 1930s (Welch 2007).

The Structure of an Argument in Southwest Culture History

We can see in Wheat's dissertation and Haury's various intellectual and logistical moves the fundamental elements of an interpretive argument in the prevailing paradigm of the era—that of culture history. The Southwest expression of this argument was somewhat different from that of other regions of North America because of several characteristics of the archaeological record. The Southwest had excellent preservation, highly visible ruins, varied and painted ceramics, absolute dating with tree rings, and a rich ethnographic record of Native Americans who remained on the land. In accordance with these requirements, Wheat set up a time-space matrix within which were defined the six branches or regional variations of the Mogollon. For the temporal dimension, he grouped local phase sequences from these branches into broad technological stages labeled Mogollon 1 through 5. These stages were then correlated with the Anasazi and Hohokam sequences. All in all, it made for a powerful argument in the culture-history idiom, which could be simplified graphically in a chart.

The argument Wheat presented rested on and was supported by the prodigious excavation and reporting of Haury, Sayles, Martin, Rinaldo, and Bluhm. At the time of Wheat's writing, the number of sites excavated and made available through standard site reports was more significant than the actual evidence, as witnessed by the negative evaluation that Bullard wrote in 1962. The scarcity of excavated sites had been an early criticism of the Mogollon concept, but by the mid-1950s, this common complaint had been erased. The importance of in-field demonstrations as an integral component of argumentation and verification has already been stressed.

Despite his oft-stated belief that archaeology was as much art as science, Haury held to the conviction that data were integral to any argument. The archaeological process—as he saw it, investigation, analysis, interpretation, and peer evaluation—was not a closed circle but an upward-looping spiral. The archaeologist must always seek fresh data. These tenets of scientific method fostered Haury's response to the Mogollon and Hohokam controversies.

Competition and Interaction

An important but heretofore understudied feature of the culture-history paradigm, which may also be an artifact of disciplinary growth, is the interaction of students among different and sometimes competing projects. Harvard students attended the field school at Point of Pines, and Arizona students participated in the Peabody Museum's Upper Gila Expedition. This degree of interaction must have been accompanied by exchange of ideas and exposure to varied archaeological remains. Of course, the exchange did not affect each student equally. Daifuku, a Harvard student at Point of Pines, did not convert to belief in the Mogollon, although his fellow students with strong Arizona ties, Danson and Wendorf, did, or at least supported in their dissertations important elements of the pro-Mogollon position.

In contrast to the heated polemics of later years pitting colleagues of different intellectual positions against each other in highly personal ways (see discussion of the Grasshopper–Chavez Pass debate in Reid and Whittlesey 2005), we can uncover very little evidence of personal animosity, certainly none between Haury and his Harvard alma mater. Haury and Kidder, a staunch opponent of the Mogollon from the beginning of the controversy, were lifelong friends and colleagues (fig. 14.1), as were Brew and Haury (Nash 1999:112). This collegiality cannot, however, be taken as a measure of the temperature of the controversy but as a protracted example of polite disputation among scholars over serious differences of interpretation. One measure of this can be seen in Haury's recollection of the 1948 Pecos Conference at Point of Pines: "Hot debates, firm stands

Figure 14.1 Alfred Vincent Kidder (left) and Emil Haury at Point of Pines Pueblo in 1948. (Photograph by E. B. Sayles; courtesy of the Arizona State Museum; neg. no. 3208)

pro and con, an earnest searching for answers, characterized the session" (Haury 1979:172).

Factors of place as well as the forces of personality may have contributed in subtle ways to the Mogollon controversy. We have wondered from time to time at what must have been a clash between the staid and conservative environs of Harvard and the Peabody Museum and the rough-and-tumble western landscapes where the academicians pitted themselves against the pit houses and pueblos of plateau and desert. Did Brew, for example, try to re-create the atmosphere of brandy and tuxedos, paneled walls and prints, cigars and Chinese porcelain of the clubby Harvard dining rooms in the comparative wilds of the Hopi Mesas? Or did the stark, flat mesas, the scrubby brush, and the incomparable skies of the West effect a subtle change in attitude and belief? We suspect the latter, although we have no recollections from Brew himself to back up our beliefs. Doing archaeology, regardless of its context, requires archaeologists to confront the intersections of place with time, environment with people, and memory with the present day.

Theoretical Paradigms

Not to be denied as a player in the Mogollon controversy and its resolution is the shifting nature of Southwest archaeology, particularly its methods and theories. As much as Haury understood the requirements of culture history and exercised academic power to enhance his argument for the existence of a Mogollon culture and thus bring to a conclusion the controversy as it was originally framed, it was a shift in the theoretical paradigm of American archaeology that kept the controversy from reigniting in the early 1960s. We have seen that, not long after Wheat's defense of the Mogollon, a new kind of archaeology was born out of the Field Museum of Natural History's field school at Vernon—processual archaeology, Arizona variety. As Haury recalled, southwestern archaeologists from the beginning had emphasized the definition of complexes and devised chronologies to accommodate them. It was this strong foundation of who, what, and when that laid the groundwork for the problems of how and why that came to occupy Longacre and also Martin in his later years. The explosion of the New Archaeology on the scene was a successful diversion from the dusty issues of Mogollon primacy and legitimacy. Frankly, not many cared by the time that Bullard and Daifuku breathed their last critical gasps in print.

By this time, Haury was caught up in yet another major controversy—that of Hohokam chronology and origins—and it would consume the remainder of his professional career. Haury's attitude toward the shifting tides of method and theory was rather casual, which is curious given the role, albeit small, that the shift played in ending the Mogollon controversy. He recalled (Haury 1979:225), "[T]he workers in the 1960s did not have a monopoly on what was good in archaeology and ... what they were doing did not render sterile all the work that had been done before. Fortunately, the methodologies and the immediate aims of science are ever changing though the philosophical premises are not."

We have catalogued the history of one of southwestern archaeology's greatest controversies and the roles played by Haury and many others in this intriguing and still-puzzling story. We have tracked the Mogollon and the scholars who studied them across the mountains and forests of Arizona and New Mexico and onto the arid plateau north of the Mogollon Rim. We have monitored the influence of paradigm shifts in Southwest archaeology and the role of people and institutions in the controversy. Our tale has demonstrated the pervasive influence of place in shaping personalities and archaeological approaches to the past. Places are not simply constructions of topography and sky, water and vegetation, animals and stone. Places are created by human practice, intention, belief, and cognition. Each place is a rich and deeply layered entity where past and present interactions with the land resonate in our hearts and our memories and shape our actions. So it was with the Mogollon controversy, we believe, and its scholars who debated in gentlemanly fashion, created intellectual agendas and arguments, and ultimately brought the controversy to an end.

Epilogue

> [O]ut of it all progress has and is being made and . . . our
> understanding of the past is continually being sharpened. As
> is usually the case when new ventures and ideas are being
> touted, the pendulum's swing at first outreaches itself only to
> settle back to record a higher mid-point, a comfortable gain.
> I delight in seeing that take place, in recognizing solid advances
> have been made and that unreachable goals are being seen
> for what they are.
>
> —Emil Haury (1979:226)

Today, the Mogollon controversy, as it was envisioned, framed, and resolved by Haury, his students, and his colleagues, is over. Since the resolution of the controversy in 1955, scholarly interest in the Mogollon concept
and its greater intellectual meaning has waxed and waned, but Mogollon
archaeology has a remarkable ability to continue to inspire us with fresh
ideas, unorthodox but unshakable interpretations of prehistory, and the
energy to strike out in new directions.

The biennial Mogollon Conference emerged in the 1980s as a forum
for Mogollon researchers to present the results of their work (Beckett
1982)—"to debate, defend and introduce new ideas with our colleagues
who shared many of the same problems" (Beckett 1991). The Mogollon
Conference has become the principal venue for discussing sites and
regions that fall within the broad geographical boundaries of the tradi-
tionally conceived Mogollon. More than that, it also has been the place for
initiating new controversies and sending up "trial balloons" for fresh ideas
that would subsequently be debated elsewhere (Reid and Whittlesey 2005;
Whittlesey 1999). The Mogollon Conference tacitly endorses the concept
of a Mogollon culture, but often does not confront the problems left dan-
gling from the past and the problems recent research has uncovered.

Although we have stated previously that the New Archaeology moved archaeologists to pursue fresh directions that were shorn of an interest in culture history per se, the Mogollon culture concept continues to be reclassified at Mogollon Conferences and elsewhere. For example, the concept was questioned at the Fourth Mogollon Conference marking the fiftieth anniversary of the Mogollon culture that was held at the University of Arizona in 1986. Speth (1988:201) and Wilcox (1988:207) argued that cultural labels such as Mogollon, Anasazi, and Hohokam deflect prehistorians from meaningful inquiry and should be abandoned.

Others have reclassified Mogollon as a variant of another cultural tradition. Wood and McAllister (1982), for example, view Hohokam and Mogollon as a single culture represented prehistorically by two archaeological traditions. They interpret the Salado culture of the Tonto Basin as a variant of the Classic period Hohokam cultural tradition. Gregory and Wilcox redefine the Mogollon as the "heuristic concept of adaptation that acts as an intervening variable between culture and environment" and argue for a "Zunian compact language community composed of populations with four different adaptations" (Gregory and Wilcox 2007:414).

Whereas we have presented evidence from Grasshopper Pueblo and adjacent archaeological sites in the Grasshopper region that the Mogollon persisted as a distinctive social identity and lifeway beyond AD 1000 into the Mogollon Pueblo period (Reid 1989; Reid and Whittlesey 1999), Mills (1999:3–4) prefers to group Mogollon and Anasazi, using the term "Ancestral Pueblo" to refer to the post–AD 1000 populations who occupied the Mogollon Rim region. In so doing, Mills subscribes to the earlier notion of "Anasazi swamping" that held sway in earlier decades.

Occasionally, some archaeologists have placed the Mogollon under a new label without changing the defining characteristics of the culture. For example, Elson, Stark, and Heidke (1992:281) call for a sub–Mogollon Rim cultural tradition extending from the Tonto Basin throughout east-central Arizona and into New Mexico that they term the Central Arizona Tradition after Wood (1989). Still others throw another ethnic wrench into the works in documenting movements of Kayenta Anasazi groups up the San Pedro River and as far south as the Safford area during the AD 1200s (Clark 2001; Lyons 2003; Woodson 1999). Of course, Haury (1958), Lindsay (1992), and Di Peso (1958) had argued for migrations into Point of Pines and the San Pedro River valley much earlier. Haury's criteria for identifying migrations in the archaeological record remain the model of this process.

The landscape of Mogollon archaeology has changed irrevocably from that of the 1930s and the decades of the Mogollon controversy. So too has American archaeology in general. Today's concerns with identity, the trappings of power, gender issues, ritual, astronomy and architecture, and other higher-order concepts discussed at recent Mogollon Conferences certainly would seem out of place in a 1950s-era site report, but the foundation for contemporary studies rests in the close attention to detail and meticulous archaeology of our predecessors. Throughout these discussions, we will continue to argue the utility of the culture concept, as discussed in chapter 1. Most contemporary peoples do not categorize themselves as "regional systems," "world systems," "macrosystems," "interaction spheres," "cults," or "phenomena" (as in Chaco Phenomenon). These are constructs invented and used by archaeologists. Whereas we may never be able to approximate a complete archaeological ethnography of an ancient people, it behooves us to think in more anthropologically viable terms and to structure our research with anthropological objectives in mind.

The future holds great promise that the Mogollon will continue to inspire students and their professors for many decades. Our story has come full circle from the pit-house villages and pueblos of the mountains to the places where a new generation of field-school students works and learns. Haury's initial formulation of the Mogollon culture has met the test of time and survived the fires of controversy that enveloped it for so long. For Haury, the discovery, definition, and defense of the Mogollon cultural concept was a lifelong pursuit from which he must have derived intense personal and intellectual satisfaction. In 1979, he recalled, "given the chance to go through it all again, I would make no basic changes in the choices I made" (Haury 1979:261). Our chronology and history of the Mogollon concept and controversy have been equally satisfying, and we hope our readers have enjoyed the retelling of this story. The continuing and changing use of the Mogollon concept in contemporary archaeological discourse surely underscores our belief that the Southwest is an extraordinary landscape and always will be an exciting venue for the interaction of personalities and places to interpret and understand the peoples and places of the past.

Appendix
Excerpt from Pat Wheat's Transcription of the Pecos Conference at Point of Pines, August 1948 (pp. 31–40)

MARTIN: Is it fair to consider Mogollon a culture?

HAURY: Hohokam and Anasazi have a number of characteristic features. It is not necessary that every group have as many distinguishing characteristics. The trait list for an Apache site will be small. The Awatovi trait list is large. We need not assume that in order to define a culture we must have something as clear-cut as Anasazi.

BREW: I agree with everything Haury said in his preliminary statement. I have walked over from the bend of the Gila south of Silver City a total of some hundreds of sites as far north as the North Plains. There is no question at all that there is a ceramic difference from other areas in the Southwest. I still feel that if you had Apache sites and didn't have Apache people you could not set up an Apache culture. One point in this disagreement is with the matter of a limitation of archaeological technique. I think that when Apache sites are found they would be of such a nature that they would not be set as a separate culture.

[Haury questions Brew on the matter of not recognizing the material evidence (31).]

COLLIER: Questions the ethnographic use of the term "Culture." Defining the term does not seem to clarify the problem, as it is used in many ways in ethnology as well as in archaeology.

BREW: We need a new definition of culture.

KIDDER: Speaking of what is a culture: everyone recognizes that something exists in this area. The point that needs consideration and investigation is what part that culture played in the Southwest as a whole. It should be related to all other phases. One of the tenets of the Mogollonists is that that culture played an important part in the development of the Southwest as a whole. If so, it is of importance. But this can only be determined by chronology and correlation. I was also opposed to Mogollon originally, but now see it as an extremely important problem. What part did the Mogollon play in the picture of development? Those problems of inter-influence and chronology are important in determining the name.

[Martin asks Lehmer to explain the map he has drawn on the blackboard.]

LEHMER: [We skip to the end of his comments (32).]

By 1000 a basic pattern was beginning to take on traditions from the north which came down. Some agree that by about 1000 Mogollon had been submerged by northern traditions coming down. Still later another push from the north by the Salado down into Hohokam country.

ERIK REED: Does not believe in the submergence theory.

AL SCHROEDER: Also objects. Thinks the Sinagua submerged the Hohokam about 1150 and the Salado came later.

Haury then called the meeting back to the original problem. [p. 33] [We skip over a page of short exchanges (33–34) on unfired pottery, independent invention, and stone tools.]

JIM HALL: Could we make a differentiation between the Mogollon problem from the Hohokam and the Anasazi, i.e., define where is the difference and what is it? (34)

HAURY: There are parallels in houses between the south and the north, but in general you will find less specialization in the south. There are some lithic differences. Too much attention is paid to Basketmaker baskets and not enough to stone tools which they must have used. Pottery still is one of the best indicators and we should make the most of it. There is too little evidence to define the group on the basis of physical type.

JIM HALL: Could we define it on pithouse types?

HAURY: No.

MARTIN: The farther you go back in time, the more similar the pithouses are, since they probably have a common origin. Specialized developments have been noted in BM 3 [Basketmaker III], such as ventilators, antechambers, slab-lined houses. As time goes on in each culture one finds more specialization. Architecture would not be enough to build an hypothesis on.

REED: Isn't the lack of distinctive features in itself a distinctive feature? How can you throw this in with Anasazi, with its distinctive features? How different does something have to be to be different?

BREW: Can't see how the fact that two things are so similar that you can't draw distinctions proves that the cultures are different. Believes that the nature of the houses that people live in and the temples in which they worship are of more importance feature of the culture than the nature of one phase of their pottery. Admits there is a very distinct ceramic difference, but wants to see something more than this.

MARTIN: Is not sure that the Mogollon had a great deal of influence on the surrounding cultures.

HAURY: Corn and pottery passed through the Mogollon area and was transmitted by the Mogollon people. Thinks Mogollon did affect northern development but not violently.

MARTIN: Thinks the Mogollon were a pretty low, simple development that can't be explained away—it did exist.

BREW: No question of a ceramic difference, but it was not important nor useful in setting up a culture. Doesn't like the equating of Mogollon in terms of culture with Pueblo and Hohokam on the basis of a single trait such as pottery differences.

HAURY: It is enough to distinguish certain Pueblo groups, though?????

O'BRYAN: Anasazi was defined. Then Hohokam was defined on the differences from Anasazi. By the time Mogollon was defined there wasn't much difference left to make a definition.

SAYLES: Is trying to establish the Mogollon as a basic pattern. It is shared with other cultures. Mogollon never did develop as high as the other cultures, especially in the geographic area in which we know it. Are we actually on the fringe of something if we say that it came from the south? Tests in Chihuahua showed a sequence of pottery types. The earliest was an early brown ware, polished brown and polished red wares. It seems that the only way we can look at Mogollon is that it is a basic pattern.

BREW: Will not define a culture on the basis of a pottery type. Wants to find out what happened. The only thing I question is what seems to be an attempt to jump the gun and to talk about a culture group on the basis of such little evidence. The thing that a large number of people objected to was this business of the concept of a distinct culture group involving other people. To have a distinct culture group you must have more evidence that just pottery.

WALT TAYLOR: Thinks the men working on the Mogollon have done the work and made their decision that they have something worthwhile. Thinks they should use pottery as a guide but should have many other distinctive features. Classification may be set up on the basis of pottery but only as a symbol of a judgment that has been set up on the basis of a great number of other things.

BREW: All right, then, what are the other things?

JIM HALL (to Brew): Would you recognize a difference in a pithouse of BM 3 and Mogollon?

BREW: Has a series of pithouses which EWH has seen, similar to the pithouses here at Point of Pines.

HAURY: The interior furnishings are consistently different.

BREW: If you can establish a difference in house types, that is a strong point. But no house type differences have been established here this morning. Everyone says you can't. I believe the Mogollon is part of a basic culture which spread all over the Southwest and is only a localized development from that basic culture.

WHITING: Should we drop "Anasazi" and call it Basketmaker-Mogollon culture?

BREW: Why did you give it a name if it is the same as the Basketmaker?

SAYLES: EWH gave it a name because he thought it was different. As we have worked back in time we find that the thing EWH first called Mogollon is actually very widespread. It is only toward the south, toward the source of these traits, that you find this basic pattern persisting into fairly late times. In the north the submergence takes place. We have P3 [Pueblo III] pithouses right here. We have other traits which may trace back into this Georgetown pithouse. (36)

[We omit the rather lengthy discussion of pithouse architectural traits that follows (36–38).]

MARTIN: Asks Brew if he would be convinced if they could show him a distinct difference in house types. (38)

BREW: If a distinct house type could be established it would be a much better argument. Have every one of these particular house types in Jeddito, so do not feel that anything has been established. My question is: If you want to say that the BM is a slightly different variation of the widespread culture, that is agreeable. It might be better to get another name which hasn't this tradition of 15 or 20 years' dispute; get another name that includes the whole business and abandon the idea of a definite difference. If the claim is that BM is Mogollon, that is agreeable.

LEHMER: At one time you have one thing; at another you have three separate things; at another time you have a coalition of two. The period around 500 is the question.

BREW: Doesn't see the point in a 3-way split on the basis of a pottery type difference. If you can add a distinct house type the argument is better. Doesn't think the dates prove the difference in house types as described on the black board.

MARTIN: It would be possible, if we had time, to give a complete list of distinctive traits which have been published. (38)

[We skip comments by Haury, Morris, and Danson (38–39).]

HAURY: At 300 A.D. we have Mogollon, clear and definite. But by 500 it is beginning to merge. By 700 it is merged. If you draw a space map from north to southeast it will be a progressive later survival. House types are confusing. I am not sure how much these differences will mean. Overlapping conditions indicate that may be there is no distinction. I am on the fence about house types. (39) [We skip over comments by Sayles, Colton, and Rinaldo (39–40) to hear the session's concluding statement by Reed.]

REED: There is actually not as much divergence as there seems. Around 850 to 900 we find [stone] surface buildings as dwellings with a definite ceremonial chamber, a gray corrugated pottery, black-on-white [pottery], pebble axes, no cranial deformation. In the Mimbres we have red ware, plain ware, red-on-brown. How can you consider that these pithouse redware groups are the same as Anasazi? (40)

Bibliography

Ambrose, Stephen E.

1996   *Undaunted Courage: Meriwether Lewis, Thomas Jefferson, and the Open-ing of the American West.* New York: Simon and Schuster.

Anyon, Roger

1980   The Late Pithouse Period. In *An Archaeological Synthesis of South Central and Southwestern New Mexico*, edited by S. A. LeBlanc and M. E. Whalen, 141–255. Albuquerque: Office of Contract Archaeology, University of New Mexico.

Anyon, Roger, and Steven A. LeBlanc

1984   *The Galaz Ruin: A Prehistoric Mimbres Village in Southwestern New Mexico.* Albuquerque: University of New Mexico Press.

Asch, C. M.

1961   Post-Pueblo Occupation of the Willow Creek Ruin, Point of Pines. *The Kiva* 26 (2): 31–42.

Ashmore, Wendy, and A. Bernard Knapp

1999   *Archaeologies of Landscape: Contemporary Perspectives.* Malden, MA: Blackwell Publishers.

Basso, Keith H.

1996   *Wisdom Sits in Places: Landscape and Language among the Western Apache.* Albuquerque: University of New Mexico Press.

Beckett, Patrick H.

1982   Introduction and Acknowledgments. In *Mogollon Archaeology: Proceedings of the 1980 Mogollon Conference*, edited by P. H. Beckett and K. Silverbird, 1–2. Ramona, CA: Acoma Books.

1991   Introduction. In *Mogollon V*, edited by P. H. Beckett and J. H. Kelly, 1–2. Las Cruces, NM: COAS Publishing and Research.

Bostwick, Todd W.

2006   *Byron Cummings: Dean of Southwest Archaeology.* Tucson: University of Arizona Press.

Breternitz, David A.

1959   *Excavations at Nantack Village, Point of Pines, Arizona.* Anthropological Papers of the University of Arizona 1. Tucson: University of Arizona Press.

Brew, John Otis

1942   Review of *Southwestern Archaeology*, by John C. McGregor. *American Antiquity* 8:191–96.

1946   *Archaeology of Alkali Ridge, Southeastern Utah*. Papers of the Peabody Museum of American Archaeology and Ethnology, Harvard University, 21. Cambridge, MA.

1968   Introduction. In *One Hundred Years of Anthropology*, edited by J. O. Brew, 5–25. Cambridge, MA: Harvard University Press.

Brew, John Otis, and Edward B. Danson

1948   The 1947 Reconnaissance and the Proposed Upper Gila Expedition of the Peabody Museum of Harvard University. *El Palacio* 55:211–22.

Brew, John Otis, and Watson Smith

1954   Comments. *American Anthropologist* 56:586–88.

Bullard, William R., Jr.

1962   *The Cerro Colorado Site and Pithouse Architecture in the Southwestern United States Prior to A.D. 900*. Papers of the Peabody Museum of American Archaeology and Ethnology, Harvard University, 44 (2). Cambridge, MA.

Burgess, Don

2009   Romans in Tucson? The Story of an Archaeological Hoax. *Journal of the Southwest* 51 (1).

Cather, Willa

1990   *Death Comes for the Archbishop*. New York: Vintage Books. (Originally published 1927.)

Clark, Jeffery J.

2001   *Tracking Prehistoric Migrations: Pueblo Settlers among the Tonto Basin Hohokam*. Anthropological Papers of the University of Arizona 65. Tucson: University of Arizona Press.

Colton, Harold S.

1939   *Prehistoric Culture Units and Their Relationships in Northern Arizona*. Museum of Northern Arizona Bulletin 17. Flagstaff: Museum of Northern Arizona.

Cordell, Linda S., and Don D. Fowler, eds.

2005   *Southwest Archaeology in the Twentieth Century*. Salt Lake City: University of Utah Press.

Daifuku, Hiroshi

1952   A New Conceptual Scheme for Prehistoric Cultures in the Southwestern United States. *American Anthropologist* 54:191–200.

1961   *Jeddito 264: A Report on the Excavation of a Basket Maker III–Pueblo I Site in Northeastern Arizona, With a Review of Some Current Theories in Southwestern Archaeology*. Papers of the Peabody Museum of American Archaeology and Ethnology, Harvard University, 33 (1). Cambridge, MA.

Danson, Edward B.

1957   *An Archaeological Survey of West Central New Mexico and East Central Arizona*. Papers of the Peabody Museum of American Archaeology and Ethnology, Harvard University, 44 (1). Cambridge, MA.

Di Peso, Charles C.

1958   *The Reeve Ruin of Southeastern Arizona: A Study of Western Pueblo Migration into the Middle San Pedro Valley*. Publication 8. Dragoon, AZ: Amerind Foundation.

Dongoske, Kurt E., Michael Yeatts, Roger Anyon, and T. J. Ferguson

1997   Archaeological Cultures and Cultural Affiliation: Hopi and Zuni Perspectives in the American Southwest. *American Antiquity* 62:600–608.

Douglass, Andrew E.

1985   Checking the Date of Bluff Ruin, Forestdale: A Study in Technique. In *Mogollon Culture in the Forestdale Valley, East-Central Arizona*, by Emil W. Haury, 427–32. Tucson: University of Arizona Press. Reprint. Originally published 1942, *Tree-Ring Bulletin* 9 (2):2–7.

Dyck, Cornelius J.

1993   *An Introduction to Mennonite History*. 3rd ed. Scottdale, PA: Herald Press.

Eggan, Fred

1968   One Hundred Years of Ethnology and Social Anthropology. In *One Hundred Years of Anthropology*, edited by J. O. Brew, 119–52. Cambridge, MA: Harvard University Press.

Elson, Mark D., Miriam T. Stark, and James M. Heidke

1992   Prelude to Salado: Preclassic Period Settlement in the Upper Tonto Basin. In *Proceedings of the Second Salado Conference, Globe, AZ, 1992*, edited by R. C. Lange and S. Germick, 274–85. Occasional Paper 2. Phoenix: Arizona Archaeological Society.

Ezzo, Joseph A., and T. Douglas Price

2002   Migration, Regional Reorganization, and Spatial Group Composition at Grasshopper Pueblo, Arizona. *Journal of Archaeological Science* 29:499–520.

Fowler, Don D.

2000   *A Laboratory for Anthropology: Science and Romanticism in the American Southwest, 1846–1930*. Albuquerque: University of New Mexico Press.

Gifford, Carol A., and Elizabeth A. Morris

1985   Digging for Credit: Early Archaeological Field Schools in the American Southwest. *American Antiquity* 50:395–411.

Gifford, James C.

1980   *Archaeological Explorations in Caves of the Point of Pines Region, Arizona*. Anthropological Papers of the University of Arizona 36. Tucson: University of Arizona Press.

Gladwin, Harold S.

1942   *Excavations at Snaketown III: Revisions*. Medallion Papers 30. Globe, AZ:
        Gila Pueblo.

1948   *Excavations at Snaketown IV: Review and Conclusions*. Medallion Papers
        38. Globe, AZ: Gila Pueblo.

Gladwin, Harold S., Emil W. Haury, E. B. Sayles, and Nora Gladwin

1937   *Excavations at Snaketown: Material Culture*. Medallion Papers 25. Globe,
        AZ: Gila Pueblo.

Gladwin, Winifred, and Harold S. Gladwin

1934   *A Method for the Designation of Cultures and Their Variations*. Medallion
        Papers 15. Globe, AZ: Gila Pueblo.

Gregory, David A., and David R. Wilcox

2007   A New Research Design for Studying Zuni Origins and Similar Anthro-
        pological Problems. In *Zuni Origins: Toward a New Synthesis of South-
        western Archaeology*, edited by D. A. Gregory and D. R. Wilcox, 407–23.
        Tucson: University of Arizona Press.

Haury, Emil W.

1936   *The Mogollon Culture of Southwestern New Mexico*. Medallion Papers 20.
        Globe, AZ: Gila Pueblo.

1940   *Excavations in the Forestdale Valley, East-Central Arizona*. University of
        Arizona Bulletin 12, Social Science Bulletin 11 (4). Tucson: University
        of Arizona.

1943   A Possible Cochise-Mogollon-Hohokam Sequence. *Proceedings of the
        American Philosophical Society* 86:260–63.

1945a   *The Excavations of Los Muertos and Neighboring Ruins in the Salt River
        Valley, Southern Arizona*. Papers of the Peabody Museum of American
        Archaeology and Ethnology, Harvard University, 24. Cambridge, MA.

1945b   The Problems of Contacts between Mexico and the Southwestern United
        States. *Southwestern Journal of Anthropology* 1 (1):55–74.

1949a   The 1948 Southwestern Archaeological Conference. *American Antiquity*
        14:254–56.

1949b   Review of *Archaeology of Alkali Ridge*, by John Otis Brew. *American Antiq-
        uity* 15:54–66.

1950a   *The Stratigraphy and Archaeology of Ventana Cave*. Tucson: University of
        Arizona Press; Albuquerque: University of New Mexico Press.

1950b   Foreword. In *A Report of the Excavation of a Small Ruin Near Point of
        Pines, East Central Arizona*, by Fred Wendorf. University of Arizona
        Bulletin 21 (3), Social Science Bulletin 19:7–10. Tucson: University of
        Arizona.

1957   An Alluvial Site of the San Carlos Indian Reservation, Arizona. *Ameri-
        can Antiquity* 23:2–27.

1958   Evidence at Point of Pines for a Prehistoric Migration from Northern

Arizona. In *Migrations in New World Culture History*, edited by R. H. Thompson, 1–8. University of Arizona Bulletin 29 (2), Social Science Bulletin 27. Tucson: University of Arizona.

1962   HH-39: Recollections of a Dramatic Moment in Southwestern Archaeology. *Tree-Ring Bulletin* 24 (2–3):11–14.

1976   *The Hohokam: Desert Farmers and Craftsmen: Excavations at Snaketown, 1964–1965.* Tucson: University of Arizona Press.

1979   Emil Walter Haury: A Personal View. Manuscript on file (oral history transcription) in the Arizona State Museum Library, University of Arizona, Tucson.

1985a   *Mogollon Culture in the Forestdale Valley, East-Central Arizona.* Tucson: University of Arizona Press.

1985b   Reflections: Fifty Years of Southwestern Archaeology. *American Antiquity* 50:383–94.

1988   Gila Pueblo Archaeological Foundation: A History and Some Personal Notes. *Kiva* 54 (1).

1989   *Point of Pines, Arizona: A History of the University of Arizona Archaeological Field School.* Anthropological Papers of the University of Arizona 50. Tucson: University of Arizona Press.

1995   Wherefore a Harvard Ph.D.? *Journal of the Southwest* 37:710–33.

2004   Cuicuilco Diary: June 11–September 12, 1925. *Journal of the Southwest* 46:55–91.

Haury, Emil W., and E. B. Sayles

1947   *An Early Pit House Village of the Mogollon Culture, Forestdale Valley, Arizona.* University of Arizona Bulletin 18 (4), Social Science Bulletin 16. Tucson: University of Arizona.

Haury, Loren R.

2004a   Introduction. Cuicuilco Diary: June 11–September 12, 1925. *Journal of the Southwest* 46:55.

2004b   Emil Haury: Art into Archaeology. *Journal of the Southwest* 46:9–18.

Heckman, Robert A., Barbara K. Montgomery, and Stephanie M. Whittlesey

2000   *Prehistoric Painted Pottery of Southeastern Arizona.* Technical Series 77. Tucson: Statistical Research, Inc.

Hodder, Ian

2003   Archaeological Reflexivity and the "Local" Voice. *Anthropological Quarterly* 76 (1):55–69.

Jackson, John B.

1984   *Discovering the Vernacular Landscape.* New Haven: Yale University Press.

Jennings, Jesse D.

1994   *Accidental Archaeologist: Memoirs of Jesse D. Jennings.* Salt Lake City: University of Utah Press.

Johnson, Alfred E.

1965   The Development of Western Pueblo Culture. PhD diss., Department of Anthropology, University of Arizona, Tucson.

Judd, Neil M.

1940   Progress in the Southwest. In *Historical Anthropology of North America*. Smithsonian Miscellaneous Collections 123, Washington, D.C.: Smithsonian Institution.

Kidder, Alfred V.

1924   *An Introduction to the Study of Southwestern Archaeology*. New Haven: Yale University Press.

1931   *The Pottery of Pecos*. New Haven: Phillips Academy.

1939   Review of *Starkweather Ruin*, by Paul H. Nesbitt. *American Anthropologist* 41:314–16.

1960   Reminiscences in Southwest Archaeology: 1. *The Kiva* 25:1–32.

Kluckhohn, Clyde M.

1972   The Conceptual Structure in Middle American Studies. In *Contemporary Archaeology: A Guide to Theory and Contributions*, edited by M. P. Leone, 78–84. Carbondale: Southern Illinois University Press.

LeBlanc, Steven A.

1986   Development of Archaeological Thought on the Mimbres Mogollon. In *Emil W. Haury's Prehistory of the American Southwest*, edited by J. J. Reid and D. E. Doyel, 297–304. Tucson: University of Arizona Press.

Lehmer, Donald J.

1948   *The Jornada Branch of the Mogollon*. University of Arizona Bulletin 19 (2), Social Science Bulletin 17. Tucson: University of Arizona.

Lindsay, Alexander J.

1992   Tucson Polychrome: History, Dating, Distribution, and Design. In *Proceedings of the Second Salado Conference. Globe, AZ 1992*, edited by R. C. Lange and S. Germick, 230–37. Occasional Paper 2. Phoenix: Arizona Archaeological Society.

Longacre, William A.

1970   *Archaeology as Anthropology: A Case Study*. Anthropological Papers of the University of Arizona 17. Tucson: University of Arizona Press.

1976   Paul Sidney Martin, 1899–1974. *American Anthropologist* 78:90–92.

Lowell, Julie C.

1991   *Prehistoric Households at Turkey Creek Pueblo, Arizona*. Anthropological Papers of the University of Arizona 54. Tucson: University of Arizona Press.

Lyons, Patrick D.

2003   *Ancestral Hopi Migrations*. Anthropological Papers of the University of Arizona 68. Tucson: University of Arizona Press.

Madson, John

1982   *Where the Sky Began: Land of the Tallgrass Prairie.* Iowa City: University of Iowa Press.

Martin, Paul Sidney

1937   Review of *The Mogollon Culture of Southwestern New Mexico,* by Emil W. Haury. *American Antiquity* 2:233–34.

1943   *The SU Site: Excavations at a Mogollon Village, Western New Mexico, 1941.* Fieldiana: Anthropology 32 (2). Chicago: Field Museum of Natural History.

1959a   *Digging into History. A Brief Account of Eighteen Years of Archaeological Work in New Mexico.* Chicago Natural History Museum Popular Series 38. Chicago: Chicago Natural History Museum.

1959b   Foreword. In *Foote Canyon Pueblo, Eastern Arizona,* by John B. Rinaldo, 149–50. Fieldiana: Anthropology 49 (2). Chicago: Field Museum of Natural History.

1961   Preface. In *Mineral Creek Site and Hooper Ranch Pueblo, Eastern Arizona,* by Paul S. Martin, John B. Rinaldo, and William A. Longacre, 3–7. Fieldiana: Anthropology 52. Chicago: Field Museum of Natural History.

1974   Early Development in Mogollon Research. In *Archaeological Researches in Retrospect,* edited by G. R. Willey, 3–29. Cambridge, MA: Winthrop Publishers.

Martin, Paul S., and Fred Plog

1973   *The Archaeology of Arizona.* Garden City, NY: Natural History Press.

Martin, Paul S., George I. Quimby, and Donald Collier

1947   *Indians before Columbus: Twenty Thousand Years of North American History Revealed by Archeology.* Chicago: University of Chicago Press.

Martin, Paul S., and John B. Rinaldo

1940   *The SU Site: Excavations at a Mogollon Village, Western New Mexico, 1939.* Fieldiana: Anthropology 32 (1). Chicago: Field Museum of Natural History.

1947   *The SU Site: Excavations at a Mogollon Village, Western New Mexico, 1946.* Fieldiana: Anthropology 32 (3). Chicago: Field Museum of Natural History.

1950a   *Sites of the Reserve Phase, Pine Lawn Valley, Western New Mexico.* Fieldiana: Anthropology 38 (3). Chicago: Field Museum of Natural History.

1950b   *Turkey Foot Ridge Site: A Mogollon Village, Pine Lawn Valley, Western New Mexico.* Fieldiana: Anthropology 38 (2). Chicago: Field Museum of Natural History.

Martin, Paul S., John B. Rinaldo, and Ernst Antevs

1949   *Cochise and Mogollon Sites, Pine Lawn Valley, Western New Mexico.* Fieldiana: Anthropology 38 (1). Chicago: Field Museum of Natural History.

Martin, Paul S., John B. Rinaldo, Elaine Bluhm, H. C. Cutler, and Roger Grange Jr.

1952   *Mogollon Cultural Continuity and Change: The Stratigraphic Analysis of*

Tularosa and Cordova Caves. Fieldiana: Anthropology 40. Chicago: Field Museum of Natural History.

Martin, Paul S., John B. Rinaldo, and William A. Longacre

1961   *Mineral Creek Site and Hooper Ranch Pueblo, Eastern Arizona.* Fieldiana: Anthropology 52. Chicago: Field Museum of Natural History.

Martin, Paul S., John B. Rinaldo, William A. Longacre, Constance Cronin, Leslie G. Freeman, Jr., and James Schoenwetter

1962   *Chapters in the Prehistory of Eastern Arizona, 1.* Fieldiana: Anthropology 53. Chicago: Field Museum of Natural History.

McGregor, John C.

1941a   *Southwestern Archaeology.* New York: John Wiley and Sons.

1941b   *Winona and Ridge Ruin: Architecture and Material Culture.* Museum of Northern Arizona Bulletin 18. Flagstaff: Museum of Northern Arizona.

1965   *Southwestern Archaeology.* 2d ed. Urbana: University of Illinois Press.

1987   Archaeological Reminiscences. Manuscript on file at Museum of Northern Arizona, Flagstaff.

Meltzer, David J.

2006   *Folsom: New Archaeological Investigations of a Classic Paleoindian Bison Kill.* Berkeley: University of California Press.

Mills, Barbara J.

1999   The Research Setting. In *Living on the Edge: Excavations and Analysis of the Silver Creek Archaeological Research Project 1993–1998,* edited by B. J. Mills, S. A. Herr, and S. Van Keuren, 1–10. Archaeological Series 192 (1). Tucson: Arizona State Museum, University of Arizona.

Mills, Barbara J., ed.

2004   *Identity, Feasting, and the Archaeology of the Greater Southwest.* Boulder: University Press of Colorado.

Morris, Earl H.

1939   *Archaeological Studies in the La Plata District, Southwestern Colorado and Northwestern New Mexico.* Carnegie Institution Publication 519. Washington, D.C.: Carnegie Institution.

Nash, Stephen E.

1999   *Time, Trees, and Prehistory: Tree-Ring Dating and the Development of North American Archaeology.* Salt Lake City: University of Utah Press.

2003   Paul Sidney Martin. In *Curators, Collections, and Contexts: Anthropology at the Field Museum, 1893–2002,* edited by S. E. Nash and G. M. Feinman, 165–77. Fieldiana: Anthropology, n.s., 36. Chicago: Field Museum of Natural History.

2006   Sites Unseen: Paul Sidney Martin's Unpublished Mogollon Excavations, 1939–1972. In *Mostly Mimbres: A Collection of Papers from the 12th Biennial Mogollon Conference,* edited by M. Thompson, J. Jurgena, and L. Jackson, 5–16. El Paso, TX: El Paso Museum of Archaeology.

Nesbitt, Paul H.
1938   *Starkweather Ruin*. Publications in Anthropology 6. Beloit, WI: Logan Museum.

Reed, Erik K.
1941   Indians Don't Stay Home. *Region Three Quarterly* 3 (4):8–9.
1942a   Implications of the Mogollon Concept. *American Antiquity* 8:27–32.
1942b   Cultural Continuities and Recombinations in the Southwest. PhD diss. (rejected), Department of Anthropology, Harvard University. Manuscript on file at the Arizona State Museum, University of Arizona, Tucson.
1943   Cultural Continuities in the Southwest. PhD diss. (rejected), Department of Anthropology, Harvard University. Manuscript on file at the Arizona State Museum, University of Arizona, Tucson.
1944   Review of *The SU Site: Excavations at a Mogollon Village, Western New Mexico, Second Season, 1941*, by Paul S. Martin and John B. Rinaldo. *American Antiquity* 9:361–63.
1946   The Distinctive Features and Distribution of San Juan Anasazi Culture. *Southwestern Journal of Anthropology* 2:295–305.
1948   The Western Pueblo Archaeological Complex. *El Palacio* 55:9–15.
1950   Eastern-Central Arizona Archaeology in Relation to the Western Pueblos. *Southwestern Journal of Anthropology* 6:120–38.
1956   Types of Village-Plan Layouts in the Southwest. In *Prehistoric Settlement Patterns in the New World*, edited by G. R. Willey, 11–17. Viking Fund Publications in Anthropology 23. New York: Wenner-Gren Foundation for Anthropological Research.

Reid, J. Jefferson
1973   Growth and Response to Stress at Grasshopper Pueblo, Arizona. PhD diss., Department of Anthropology, University of Arizona, Tucson.
1978   Response to Stress at Grasshopper Pueblo, Arizona. In *Discovering Past Behavior: Experiments in the Archaeology of the American Southwest*, edited by P. F. Grebinger, 195–213. London: Gordon and Breach.
1989   A Grasshopper Perspective on the Mogollon of the Arizona Mountains. In *Dynamics of Southwest Prehistory*, edited by L. S. Cordell and G. J. Gumerman, 65–97. Washington, D.C.: Smithsonian Institution Press.
1998   Return to Migration, Population Movement, and Ethnic Identity in the American Southwest: A Peer Reviewer's Thoughts on Archaeological Inference. In *Vanishing River: Landscapes and Lives of the Lower Verde Valley: The Lower Verde Archaeological Project*, edited by S. M. Whittlesey, R. S. Ciolek-Torrello, and J. H. Altschul, 629–38. Tucson: SRI Press.
2008   History of the Papaguería Project, 1938–1942. In *Fragile Patterns: The Archaeology of the Western Papaguería*, edited by J. H. Altschul and A. G. Rankin, 105–20. Tucson: SRI Press.

Reid, J. Jefferson, and David E. Doyel, eds.

1986   *Emil W. Haury's Prehistory of the American Southwest.* Tucson: University of Arizona Press.

Reid, J. Jefferson, and Stephanie M. Whittlesey

1982   Households at Grasshopper Pueblo. *American Behavioral Scientist* 25:687–703.

1997   *The Archaeology of Ancient Arizona.* Tucson: University of Arizona Press.

1999   *Grasshopper Pueblo: A Story of Archaeology and Ancient Life.* Tucson: University of Arizona Press.

2005   *Thirty Years into Yesterday: A History of Archaeology at Grasshopper Pueblo.* Tucson: University of Arizona Press.

Rinaldo, John B.

1941   Conjectures on the Independent Development of the Mogollon Culture. *American Antiquity* 7:5–19.

1959   *Foote Canyon Pueblo, Eastern Arizona.* Fieldiana: Anthropology 49 (2). Chicago: Field Museum of Natural History.

Roberts, Frank H. H., Jr.

1937   Archaeology in the Southwest. *American Antiquity* 3 (1).

Royce, Anya Peterson

2002   Learning to See, Learning to Listen: Thirty-Five Years of Fieldwork with the Isthmus Zapotec. In *Chronicling Cultures: Long-Term Field Research in Anthropology*, edited by R. V. Kemper and A. P. Royce, 8–33. Walnut Creek, CA: AltaMira Press.

Sayles, Edwin B.

1936   *An Archaeological Survey of Chihuahua, Mexico.* Medallion Papers 22. Globe, AZ: Gila Pueblo.

Sayles, Edwin B., and Ernst Antevs

1941   *The Cochise Culture.* Medallion Papers 29. Globe, AZ: Gila Pueblo.

Scheiber, Laura L.

2008   Intersecting Landscapes in Northeastern Colorado: A Case Study from the Donovan Site. In *Archaeological Landscapes on the High Plains*, edited by L. L. Scheiber and B. J. Clark, 17–40. Boulder: University Press of Colorado.

Seton, Ernest Thompson

1962   *Two Little Savages.* New York: Dover Publications. Originally published 1903.

Shaeffer, James Ball

1954   The Mogollon Complex: Its Cultural Role and Historical Development in the American Southwest. PhD diss., Department of Anthropology, Columbia University.

Smith, Hale G.

1949   Review of *The Jornada Branch of the Mogollon*, by Donald J. Lehmer. *American Antiquity* 15:67–68.

Smith, Watson
1952   *Excavations in Big Hawk Valley, Wupatki National Monument, Arizona.*
        Museum of Northern Arizona Bulletin 24. Flagstaff: Museum of North-
        ern Arizona.
Snead, James E.
2001   *Ruins and Rivals: The Making of Southwest Archaeology.* Tucson: Uni-
        versity of Arizona Press.
Sonnichsen, C. L.
1982   *Tucson: The Life and Times of an American City.* Norman: University of
        Oklahoma Press.
Speth, John D.
1988   Do We Need Concepts Like "Mogollon," "Anasazi," and "Hoho-
        kam" Today? A Cultural Anthropological Perspective. *The Kiva* 53:201–
        4.
Steen, Charlie R.
1981   The Life and Times of Erik Kellerman Reed. In *Collected Papers in Honor
        of Erik Kellerman Reed,* edited by A. H. Schroeder, 1–14. Archaeological
        Society of New Mexico Papers 6. Albuquerque: Albuquerque Archaeo-
        logical Society Press.
Steward, Julian H.
1955   *Theory of Culture Change: The Methodology of Multilinear Evolution.*
        Urbana: University of Illinois Press.
Taylor, Walter W.
1948   *A Study of Archeology.* American Anthropological Association Memoir
        69. Menasha, WI: American Anthropological Association.
1954   Southwestern Archaeology, Its History and Theory. *American Anthro-
        pologist* 56:561–70.
Thompson, Raymond H.
1983   Introduction. In *The Cochise Cultural Sequence in Southeastern Arizona,*
        by Edwin B. Sayles, 1–5. Anthropological Papers of the University of Ari-
        zona 42. Tucson: University of Arizona Press.
1995   Emil W. Haury and the Definition of Southwestern Archaeology. *Amer-
        ican Antiquity* 60:640–60.
2005   Anthropology at the University of Arizona, 1893–2005. *Journal of the
        Southwest* 47:327–74.
Wasley, William W., and Alfred E. Johnson
1965   *Salvage Archaeology in Painted Rocks Reservoir, Western Arizona.* Anthro-
        pological Papers of the University of Arizona 9. Tucson: University of
        Arizona Press.
Wedel, Peter J.
1954   *The Story of Bethel College.* North Newton, KS: Mennonite Press.

Welch, John R.

2007   "A Monument to Native Civilization": Byron Cummings' Still-Unfolding Vision for Kinishba Ruins. *Journal of the Southwest* 49:1–94.

Wendorf, Fred

1950   *A Report on the Excavation of a Small Ruin Near Point of Pines, East Central Arizona.* University of Arizona Bulletin 21 (3), Social Science Bulletin 19. Tucson: University of Arizona.

1953   *Archaeological Studies in the Petrified Forest National Monument.* Flagstaff: Museum of Northern Arizona.

2008   *Desert Days: My Life as a Field Archaeologist.* Dallas, TX: Southern Methodist University Press.

Wheat, Joe Ben

1952   Prehistoric Water Sources of the Point of Pines Area. *American Antiquity* 17:185–96.

1954a   *Crooked Ridge Village (Arizona W:10:15).* University of Arizona Bulletin 25 (3), Social Science Bulletin 24. Tucson: University of Arizona.

1954b   Southwestern Cultural Interrelationships and the Question of Area Co-tradition. *American Anthropologist* 56:576–86.

1955   *Mogollon Culture Prior to A.D. 1000.* Memoir 82, American Anthropological Association; Memoir 10, Society for American Archaeology. Menasha, WI: American Anthropological Association; Salt Lake City: Society for American Archaeology.

Wheat, Pat

1948   Notes on Southwestern Archaeological Conference, August, 1948. Manuscript on file at the Pecos Conference Archives, Laboratory of Anthropology, Santa Fe, NM.

1951   Pecos Archaeological Conference, August 14–17, 1951. Manuscript on file at the Pecos Conference Archives, Laboratory of Anthropology, Santa Fe, NM.

Whitehill, Walter Muir

1969   *Analecta Biographica: A Handful of New England Portraits.* Brattleboro, VT: Stephen Greene Press.

Whittlesey, Stephanie M.

1978   Status and Death at Grasshopper Pueblo: Experiments toward an Archaeological Theory of Correlates. PhD diss., Department of Anthropology, University of Arizona, Tucson.

1998   Landscape and Lives along the Lower Verde River. In *Vanishing River: Landscape and Lives of the Lower Verde Valley; The Lower Verde Archaeological Project,* edited by S. M. Whittlesey, R. S. Ciolek-Torrello, and J. H. Altschul, 703–21. Tucson: SRI Press.

1999   Preface. In *Sixty Years of Mogollon Archaeology: Papers from the Ninth*

Mogollon Conference, Silver City, New Mexico, 1996, edited by S. M. Whittlesey, vii–xiv. Tucson SRI Press.

2003   *Rivers of Rock: Stories from a Stone-Dry Land; Central Arizona Project Archaeology*. Tucson: SRI Press.

2004a   Theoretical Framework: Cultural Landscapes. In *Pots, Potters, and Models: Archaeological Investigations at the SRI Locus of the West Branch Site, Tucson, Arizona*, edited by S. M. Whittlesey, 2:181–90. Technical Series 80. Tucson: Statistical Research, Inc.

2004b   Rincon Phase Polychrome Ceramics. In *Pots, Potters, and Models: Archaeological Investigations at the SRI Locus of the West Branch Site, Tucson, Arizona*, edited by S. M. Whittlesey, 2:333–75. Technical Series 80. Tucson: Statistical Research, Inc.

Whittlesey, Stephanie M., Richard S. Ciolek-Torrello, and Jeffrey H. Altschul, eds.

1998   *Vanishing River: Landscape and Lives of the Lower Verde Valley: The Lower Verde Archaeological Project*. Tucson: SRI Press.

Whittlesey, Stephanie M., and J. Jefferson Reid

1982   Cholla Project Perspectives on Salado. In *Cholla Project Archaeology: Introduction and Special Studies*, edited by J. J. Reid, 63–80. Archaeological Series 161 (1). Tucson: Arizona State Museum, University of Arizona.

Wilcox, David R.

1988   Rethinking the Mogollon Concept. *The Kiva* 53:205–9.

2005   Creating a Firm Foundation: The Early Years of the Arizona State Museum. *Journal of the Southwest* 47:375–410.

Willey, Gordon R.

1988   *Portraits in American Archaeology*. Albuquerque: University of New Mexico Press.

Wood, J. Scott

1989   *Vale of Tiers, Too: Late Classic Period Salado Settlement Patterns and Organizational Models for Tonto Basin*. Cultural Resources Inventory Report 89-12-280. Phoenix: Tonto National Forest.

Wood, J. Scott, and Martin E. McAllister

1982   The Salado Tradition: An Alternative View. In *Cholla Project Archaeology: Introduction and Special Studies*, edited by J. J. Reid, 81–94. Archaeological Series 161 (1). Tucson: Arizona State Museum, University of Arizona.

Woodbury, Richard B.

1961   *Prehistoric Agriculture at Point of Pines, Arizona*. Society for American Archaeology Memoir 17. Salt Lake City: Society for American Archaeology.

1990   Obituary: John Otis Brew, 1906–1988. *American Antiquity* 55:452–59.

1993   *Sixty Years of Southwestern Archaeology: A History of the Pecos Conference*. Albuquerque: University of New Mexico Press.

Woodson, M. Kyle
1999   Migrations in Late Anasazi Prehistory: The Evidence from the Goat Hill
        Site. *The Kiva* 65:63–84.
Wormington, H. M.
1947   *Prehistoric Indians of the Southwest.* Denver: Colorado Museum of Nat-
        ural History.

Index

About the Authors

Jefferson Reid and Stephanie Whittlesey are professional archaeologists who specialize in writing about archaeology and ancient history for the general reader. This is their fourth book about archaeology and ancient life in prehistoric Arizona. The first book, *The Archaeology of Ancient Arizona*, published by the University of Arizona Press, introduces the history of Arizona archaeology and the prehistoric cultures of vanished Arizona. It sets the stage for a closer look at the Mogollon people of Grasshopper Pueblo, offered in their second book, *Grasshopper Pueblo: A Story of Archaeology and Ancient Life*, also published by the University of Arizona Press. Their third book, *Thirty Years into Yesterday: A History of Archaeology at Grasshopper Pueblo*, discusses the University of Arizona Archaeological Field School tradition as exemplified by thirty years of fieldwork at Grasshopper. The story presented here highlights the process of discovery in archaeology and the controversies that result by looking closely at Emil W. Haury's formulation of the Mogollon culture concept and his strategy to prove its usefulness in historical reconstructions.

Jefferson Reid is a University Distinguished Professor in the School of Anthropology at the University of Arizona, from which he received his PhD in 1973. He was director (1979–1992) of the University of Arizona Field School at Grasshopper and editor of *American Antiquity*, the scholarly journal of the Society for American Archaeology. His forty years of fieldwork range from large prehistoric pueblos of the American Southwest to temple mounds in the Southeast and Mayan pyramids in the Mexican jungle. His research interests include the method, theory, and philosophy of reconstructing past human behavior and culture; the Mogollon culture of the Arizona mountains; the historical period of southern Arizona; and especially the fascinating history of southwestern archaeology.

Stephanie Whittlesey holds a PhD in anthropology from the University of Arizona (1978). She was associated for many years with the Field School at Grasshopper. In the 1970s, she became immersed in the field of cultural resource management and has dedicated her career to meshing the goals of reconstructing the past and preserving it for future generations. Along the way, she discovered the vital importance of involving the public in archaeology. She pioneered the applications of cultural landscape studies in Southwest archaeology, as reflected in *Rivers of Rock: Stories from a Stone-Dry Land; Central Arizona Project Archaeology*, which was written for a general audience and is distributed by the University of Arizona Press. Her research interests include Native American ceramics, Mesoamerica–American Southwest connections, social organization, and the Mogollon and Hohokam cultures of Arizona's mountains and deserts.

Prehistory, Personality, and Place